SIMPLE CUISINE

BEVERLEY SUTHERLAND SMITH

SIMPLE CUISINE

DELICIOUS MEALS
IN NEXT TO NO TIME

VIKING O'NEIL

PUBLISHER'S NOTE

While more than half the recipes in this book are new, others appeared
in a different form in *A Taste in Time* (Lansdowne Press, Sydney,
1981). These recipes, in turn, have been extensively revised and
rewritten for this edition to reflect subsequent culinary changes.

Viking O'Neil
Penguin Books Australia Ltd
487 Maroondah Highway, PO Box 257
Ringwood, Victoria 3134, Australia
Penguin Books Ltd
Harmondsworth, Middlesex, England
Viking Penguin, A Division of Penguin Books USA Inc.
375 Hudson Street, New York, New York 10014, USA
Penguin Books Canada Limited
10 Alcorn Avenue, Toronto, Ontario, Canada M4V 3B2
Penguin Books (N.Z.) Ltd
182–190 Wairau Road, Auckland 10, New Zealand

First published by Penguin Books Australia Ltd 1993

10 9 8 7 6 5 4 3 2

Copyright © Beverley Sutherland Smith, 1993

Produced by Viking O'Neil
56 Claremont Street, South Yarra, Victoria 3141, Australia
A Division of Penguin Books Australia Ltd

Typeset in Sabon by Bookset, Melbourne
Photography by Les Horvat
Illustrations by Lorraine Ellis
Printed and bound through Bookbuilders Limited, Hong Kong

National Library of Australia
Cataloguing-in-Publication data

Sutherland Smith, Beverley.
   Simple cuisine: delicious meals in next to no time.

   Includes index.
   ISBN 0 670 90646 8.

   1. Cookery. 2. Quick and easy cookery. I. Sutherland Smith,
   Beverley. Taste in time. II. Title.

641.555

FRONT COVER

Fresh fruit salad, Prawns Cipriani (page 20), and Lamb Fillets with
Redcurrant and Mint (page 88) served with Sautéd Potato Cubes
(page 140) and sliced Snow Peas (page 143).

CONTENTS

INTRODUCTION

I am always surprised that busy people often resort to buying take-away food or packaged or frozen products when it only takes a little imagination (rather than a lot of time) to prepare a tasty meal.

Some years ago, with this thought in mind, I began a series of cooking classes entitled 'The Sixty Minute Gourmet'. My aim was to teach those busy people how to prepare three-course meals within an hour. The classes were a study in time and motion: I taught how corners could be cut, which dishes were suitable and which were far too time-consuming to contemplate. The classes proved very popular; so popular, indeed, that a collection of recipes used in the classes was published (*A Taste in Time*, Lansdowne Press, 1981) and became a best-seller. Completely rewritten to reflect the many culinary changes of the intervening years, *Simple Cuisine* is a revised, reformatted and considerably expanded version of that earlier book (half the recipes, in fact, are new, as is the photography).

The 'tricks' and the short cuts I taught in those early classes also form the basis of this new book. Meat, for example, has to be chosen differently when you are cooking against the clock. A leg of lamb is a slow dish; the same leg boned and butterflied can be cooked to perfection in about 45 minutes. The sauces I give here are fresh, rather than slow reductions; vegetables are stir-fried or prepared with a simple sauce. The simple addition of herbs now commonplace in most supermarkets and all markets brings a lovely flavour and colour to a dish. Fish is presented as fillets or whole, if small, and can be grilled or baked. To save time, chicken can be cut into portions or flattened for baking.

The recipes in this book are not 'store-cupboard recipes'. Instead they are reliant on fresh, seasonal produce that needs minimal preparation and cooking to create beautiful and delicious dishes.

A NOTE BEFORE COOKING

Along with the quick recipes and the time-saving tips you'll find in this book there are some additional things I find helpful to know when producing quick-and-easy meals.

- You don't need a lot of kitchen equipment, but sharp knives and a good chopping board are essential in every kitchen. A food processor is required for a few of the dishes.

- Read the recipe through before you start and follow the steps in the order given. Each recipe has been tested to ensure that the preparation time is kept to a minimum.

- When shopping get as much done as possible by the butcher, fishmonger, and so on. Ask for meat to be trimmed or minced, get chicken cut into portions, have the fish cleaned, scaled and filleted, and buy peeled prawns – all these things save your time.

- Trim vegetables a little in advance and store them in a covered container.

- Garnishes and other extras can often be prepared ahead of time. Check the recipe to see if you can whip cream, grate chocolate, brown nuts, and so on.

- Although these dishes have been designed so that their preparation and cooking can be done quickly, some can be prepared in advance and left ready for reheating.

- The base for French dressing can be made in advance. Mix oil and vinegar but don't add extra flavourings, such as mustard or garlic, as these may deteriorate and spoil the fresh flavour of the dressing. Just give it a good shake before using.

- Fresh herbs can be bought from markets, good greengrocers and many supermarkets and can be used to decorate or add flavour to the simplest seasonal food. During the winter, when fresh herbs are harder to find, you can substitute dried herbs in some dishes (try drying your own, too, when they're in season).

- Canned food used in conjunction with fresh foods can assist in the preparation of a quick meal. I buy canned pimentos (or red capsicum) imported from Spain. The colourful pimentos give a smoky flavour to dishes and are a quick substitute for the home-grilled or prepared capsicum. Be careful, however, not to use pimentos steeped in vinegar as the vinegar will sour the dish.

  I make a marvellous first course with much-neglected canned sardines coated in a vinaigrette. Canned chicken broth is an excellent base for a fast soup, while tuna, salmon and some canned fruits in syrup are useful items to keep on hand.

- Use your freezer efficiently and you'll be able to save lots of time. Leftover stale bread can be turned into breadcrumbs in a food processor; breadcrumbs can be stored in the freezer. I make a reduced chicken stock and freeze it in tiny containers once every couple of months. I just melt frozen stock over a low heat and add water to it for soups or sauces.

  Chopped frozen onion, mentioned in a few recipes, can be found in the freezer section of most supermarkets. It is mild, however, so in some cases the time spent chopping a fresh one is necessary for a tastier result.

  You can freeze passionfruit pulp in ice-cube containers; remove the cubes and wrap them in foil for storage in the freezer. I also freeze tablespoon amounts of green peppercorns wrapped in foil. Pine nuts can be browned and frozen ready for use too.

- Be consistent and careful when measuring ingredients. The metric cup (250 ml) should be used in all the recipes in this book. Where eggs are included I tested with a size 61 g.

SPRING

Appearing with the first fragile drifts of blossom, the
palest green asparagus, tiny sweet-tasting peas, new
potatoes with papery skins, pale-pink lamb and tender veal
indicate that spring and the warmer weather have arrived.
I usually like these offerings very simply cooked and
presented, the success of each dish being due to the early
perfection and freshness of the new season's produce.

FIRST COURSES

Clam and Tomato Soup

Serves 4

2 tablespoons oil
¾ cup chopped frozen onion
1 red capsicum
2 cloves garlic
½ cup dry white wine
1 × 450-g can tomatoes
½ teaspoon dried thyme *or* 2
  teaspoons fresh thyme
1 × 290-g can clams
1 teaspoon sugar
dash of Tabasco *or* cayenne pepper
  (optional)
a little cream
finely chopped fresh parsley

This is a quickly made, bright red soup that uses canned tomatoes and clams. The taste is not fishy but very fresh.

- Heat the oil in a saucepan, add the onion and leave to cook for a few minutes.

- Chop the capsicum into small pieces and discard the seeds. Chop the garlic. Add to the pan with the onion and fry for about 2 minutes.

- Add the wine, tomatoes and thyme to the pan, and cover. Leave to simmer for 10 minutes.

- Purée the tomato mixture in a blender or food processor. Return to the saucepan, add the clams and all their liquid, the sugar and heat again.

- If you like a spicy soup you can season with a dash of Tabasco or cayenne pepper.

- Pour the soup into soup bowls and trickle 1 to 2 teaspoons of cream into the centre. Top with a little parsley.

Corn and Chicken Soup

Serves 4

1 tablespoon peanut oil
2 slices fresh ginger, finely chopped
1 clove garlic, finely chopped
3 cups chicken stock
1 × 310-g can creamed corn
1 × 125-g chicken breast
4 spring onions, finely sliced
1 large egg
dash of Tabasco *or* chilli sauce

This soup is a short-cut version of a Chinese favourite. You can use the tetra packs of liquid chicken stock or canned stock.

- Heat the oil in a saucepan, add the ginger and garlic and fry for 30 seconds.

- Pour the stock into the pan, add the corn and bring to the boil.

- Cut the chicken breast into small dice or strips, add to the stock, and cook over a low heat for 1 minute.

- Add the spring onion and cook for 1 minute.

- Beat the egg and stir into the soup with a fork. It will form small pieces of egg.

- Add the Tabasco to the soup and leave to rest for 1 minute for the flavours to mellow before serving.

NOTE The soup can be reheated if you wish, but be sure to just warm again so you keep the chicken breast moist and succulent.

Asparagus with Orange-flavoured Eggs   *Serves 4*

500 g asparagus
salt
4 large eggs
grated rind of 1 orange
⅓ cup orange juice
pepper
60 g butter

How much asparagus you need depends to some extent on whether the stalks are thick or thin and whether they need peeling. Allow extra if the stalks are heavy and you need to discard quite a bit from the base.

- Bend the asparagus and snap off the tough ends. Discard. With a vegetable peeler or knife peel up the stalks towards the second-last tip.

- Three-quarter fill a large deep frying pan with water. Season, and when boiling add the asparagus stalks with the tips facing the same way. Cook, uncovered, for 8 to 12 minutes, depending on their thickness. Remove carefully and drain on a tea towel or napkin.

- Place the eggs, orange rind, juice and a little salt and pepper in a basin and beat with a fork.

- When the asparagus is partly cooked, melt the butter in a frying pan, add the egg mixture and stir constantly until it is creamy and beginning to set. The egg continues cooking even when the pan is removed, so remove the pan from the heat while the egg is still soft.

- Arrange the warm asparagus on plates, have the tips all facing the same way and spoon the egg across the stalks.

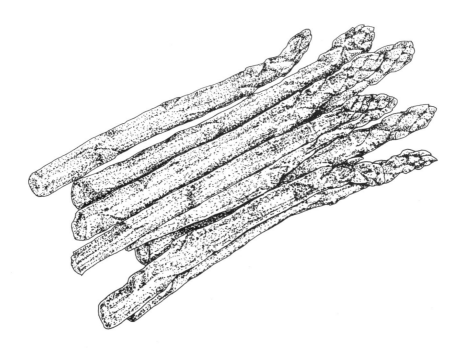

Stir-fried Asparagus and Onion

Serves 4

1 kg asparagus
2 white onions
60 g butter
salt
pepper
¾ cup chicken stock *or* water

Stir-frying keeps the asparagus crisp and green. This dish is so delicious that it should be a course on its own but it is also an ideal accompaniment to a simple chicken or meat dish. I peel the asparagus when cooking it this way so it will be tender and I usually buy thick stalks rather than pencil-thin ones.

A frying pan or wok can be used for this dish but not a saucepan; the asparagus will become wilted and soft instead of retaining its green colour and crunchy texture.

- Bend the asparagus and snap off the tough ends. Discard. With a vegetable peeler, or knife peel up the stalks towards the second-last tip. Cut into long diagonal slices, leaving the tips whole.

- Cut the onions into halves and then into thin half-slices.

- Melt the butter in a frying pan, add the onion and cook quickly for a few minutes until slightly wilted. Push to one side.

- Add the asparagus and cook for about 5 minutes in the butter. Season, and add the stock or water over the heat. Cook rapidly so most of the liquid has evaporated by the time the asparagus is tender. If the asparagus is still too firm, add a spoonful or two of water and cook until tender.

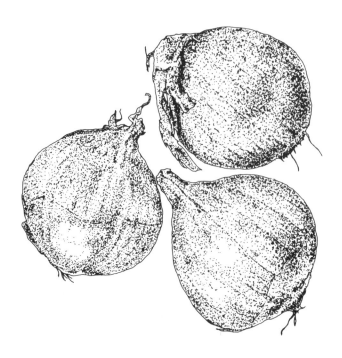

Stuffed Mushrooms Maui

Serves 4

STUFFING
2 hard-boiled eggs
90 g bacon, rind removed
1 tablespoon mayonnaise
3 tablespoons finely chopped fresh
  parsley
1 tablespoon desiccated coconut
1 tablespoon curry powder
a little milk *or* cream (if necessary)

MUSHROOMS
2 large flattish mushrooms (about
  60 g each)
30 g butter
1 tablespoon light olive oil
salt
pepper

This dish is named after the island of Maui, the second largest in the Hawaiian islands. Part of Maui is crowded with tourists, and hotels and condominiums soar into the sky. The other end of the island has retained its unspoiled atmosphere. Stuffed Mushrooms Maui was served as a small appetiser with a potent rum punch one evening during my stay at Hana Maui Hotel. Using larger mushrooms, the dish makes an exotic first course.

- Mash the eggs with a fork.

- Cut the bacon into strips and fry in a frying pan until the fat is transparent and the bacon is crisp. Drain on kitchen paper.

- Mix the bacon with the egg and add all the remaining Stuffing ingredients. If not moist you can add a little milk or cream.

- Remove the stalks from the mushrooms and discard.

- Heat the butter and oil and brush the outside of the mushrooms; this will prevent them from wrinkling and drying, which makes them tough and unattractive.

- Place the mushrooms in a greased shallow dish in which they will fit in one layer.

- Fill the mushrooms with the stuffing, taking it to the edge.

- Preheat the oven to 180°C. Bake the mushrooms for 12 to 15 minutes or until the stuffing is piping hot and the mushrooms have softened.

Smoked Fish with Avocado Sauce

Serves 4

250–375 g smoked trout
4 lettuce leaves
1 avocado (about 250 g)
2 tablespoons lemon juice
2 tablespoons mayonnaise
salt
pepper
a little cream *or* milk (if necessary)

The avocado sauce is a soft, pretty green and adds colour to the paleness of smoked trout. It should only be made about 30 minutes before use, as the avocado discolours if kept too long. This dish is quite rich so serve small portions along with some brown bread and butter wedges.

- Remove the skin and bones from the smoked trout.

- Place a lettuce leaf on four plates and arrange pieces of the trout on top.

- Cut the avocado in half and separate. Remove the stone and cut the avocado into large chunks. Purée in a food processor or mash with a fork on a dinner plate, and add the lemon juice, mayonnaise and salt and pepper. If too thick, thin with a little cream or milk.

- Coat the fish generously with the sauce.

Natural Oysters with Sour Cream and Caviar   *Serves 4*

4 dozen oysters
³/₄ cup sour cream
2 teaspoons finely grated white
   onion
1 tablespoon tomato sauce
2 teaspoons lemon juice
salt
pepper
dash of Tabasco
60 g red caviar

If you can persuade the fish shop to open the oysters fresh for you so much the better. Unfortunately, most oysters are opened well in advance and rinsed to remove all the sand, but a sauce such as this will add sparkle to any oysters.

- Remove the oysters from their shells and place aside.

- Mix the sour cream with the onion, tomato sauce, lemon juice, salt, pepper and Tabasco. Place a little of this cream in the base of each shell and replace an oyster on top. The cream can be made hours in advance but for the freshest flavour assemble the cream and oysters in the shells when you are ready to serve.

- Top with caviar and serve immediately with strips of brown bread and butter. Black caviar can be used but it can leak a grey colour over the oysters, which is not attractive, so I prefer to use the red.

Mexican Tuna with Tomato and Chilli   *Serves 4*

1 × 400-g can tuna in oil
1 red Spanish *or* mild onion, finely
   chopped
2 tomatoes, finely chopped
1 chilli, finely chopped *or* 1
   teaspoon chilli sauce
juice of ½ lemon
salt
pepper
½ cup sprigs coriander, roughly
   chopped
1 medium-sized avocado

Canned tuna is used in this dish, which is based on one a Mexican friend gave me. The sharp tang of lemon mingles with the hot chilli and aromatic coriander, cutting the richness of the tuna. I serve it with corn chips or tortillas, which can be found in the frozen-food section of specialist grocery shops. The tortillas need to be warmed with a little oil in a frying pan or brushed with oil and heated in the oven. As they are usually large, cut them into quarters and arrange around the tuna dish.

- Spread the tuna in a thin layer on an oval serving plate.

- Mix the onion in a basin with the tomato, chilli, lemon juice, salt, pepper and ¼ cup of the coriander sprigs. Taste very carefully and adjust; it should have a light lemon freshness.

- Peel the avocado, cut into dice and gently fold through the onion mixture.

- Spread the avocado mixture in a layer covering the tuna.

- Scatter the remaining coriander sprigs on top.

NOTE If preparing the dish in advance, you can make the topping but leave the avocado until close to serving. It may become rather wet as it stands, so drain away a little of the liquid if you wish.

Bean Salad with Prawns

Serves 4

500 g baby green stringless beans
salt
4 tablespoons light olive oil
1 tablespoon walnut oil
1½ tablespoons red *or* white wine
  vinegar
½ teaspoon sugar
1 teaspoon Dijon mustard
500 g peeled, cooked prawns
freshly ground black pepper

Young stringless beans make a beautiful salad, which becomes a luxury dish with a topping of prawns. Only a little walnut oil is needed to give the dressing a rich nutty flavour. Although you can cook the beans in advance, add the dressing no more than 30 minutes before serving or the vinegar in it will dull and change the bouncy green colour of the beans.

- Heat a large saucepan containing plenty of water. Top and tail the beans and when the water is boiling add them, a handful at a time, so the water comes back to the boil quickly. Season with salt, and cook rapidly until just tender. Taste to check. Drain the beans well and refresh quickly with a little cold water.

- Mix both the oils in a basin and add the vinegar, sugar and mustard. Whisk gently.

- Cut each prawn into two or three chunky pieces.

- When ready to serve, arrange the beans on a platter and scatter the prawns on top. Stir the dressing again and pour over the dish. Grind some black pepper on top.

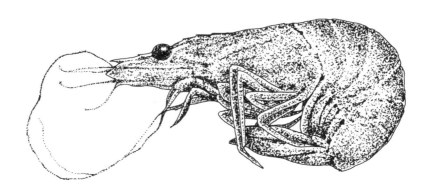

Prawns with Almond Garlic Butter

Serves 4

16 unshelled green prawns
125 g butter
3 tablespoons finely chopped fresh
  parsley
1 large clove garlic, crushed
pepper
2 teaspoons lemon juice
45 g ground almonds

I have very fond memories of prawns, split and filled with a herby butter and grilled, eaten in picturesque little restaurants in Europe. They can easily be made at home. You need to buy big fat prawns of the same size. Rather than relying on weight, allow so many per person. (See colour plate opposite.)

- Remove the heads and legs from the prawns. Carefully halve the prawns through the centre lengthwise but cut only to the shell, not through it. Turn each prawn over and using a rolling pin bang very gently so it is flattened. Turn over and remove the intestinal vein.

- Mash or process the butter with all the remaining ingredients.

- Spread a layer of the mashed butter over the flesh of each prawn, dipping the knife into hot water first so the butter will spread easily. Refrigerate the prawns.

- When ready to cook, put the prawns, butter side up, onto a tray that will fit under the grill, and cook for 5 minutes or until the prawns are cooked through. If any butter has melted away spoon it back over the top of the prawns when you serve them.

- Serve the dish with a knife and fork so the flesh of the prawns can be pulled away from the shell, and provide a small spoon for scooping up the buttery juices.

OPPOSITE PAGE ▶
Served with a side salad, Prawns with Almond Garlic Butter makes a perfect spring first course (this page).

MAIN COURSES

Racks of Lamb with Piquant Sauce
Serves 4

4 racks of lamb (4 chops each)
2 cloves garlic
freshly ground black pepper

SAUCE
2 tablespoons white wine vinegar
2 tablespoons water
3 egg yolks
60 g butter
2 tablespoons finely chopped fresh
  parsley
2 teaspoons French mustard
1 tablespoon finely chopped
  sweet-sour cucumber *or* dill
  cucumber
salt
pepper

The mustard and sweet-sour cucumber combination may seem unusual with lamb but is interesting and very piquant. You can make the sauce while the lamb is cooking and leave it at room temperature. It will be just warm, which is the best way to serve it. (See colour plate opposite.)

The sauce is an egg-based one so it is important not to let it boil or the mixture will curdle. If it is becoming too hot, remove from the heat, add all the butter quickly and whisk rapidly, which will cool it quickly.

- Remove any excess fat from the lamb and wrap a piece of foil around the bones to prevent charring.

- Cut the garlic into thick slivers. Make slashes between the bones of the racks and insert a sliver in each. Season the lamb with the freshly ground black pepper.

- Preheat the oven to 200°C. Put the meat directly on the oven rack and place a tray underneath to catch any drips. Cook for about 10 minutes, turn the oven down to 180°C and cook for a further 10 to 15 minutes or until the lamb is cooked. The timing depends on the size of the racks, but the meat should be pink on the bone.

- Remove the lamb from the oven, wrap in foil, and leave to rest for 10 minutes.

- To make the Sauce, put the vinegar and water into a small saucepan. Cook until it has reduced to about 1 tablespoon.

- Whisk the egg yolks in a small basin, whisk in the vinegar mixture and return to the saucepan, off the heat.

- Cut the butter into tiny pieces.

- Return the saucepan to the heat, add half the butter and whisk constantly until the butter has melted. If it becomes too hot lift the pan from the heat. Add more butter as it warms and the sauce thickens, then the remaining butter. It should be a creamy sauce, the texture of mayonnaise.

- Add the parsley, mustard and cucumber and stir. Taste for seasoning.

- To serve, either leave the racks whole or cut between the bones and serve individual chops. Add a little sauce to the chops and serve the rest of the sauce separately.

◄   *OPPOSITE PAGE*
Rack of Lamb with Piquant Sauce (this page), served with Baby Squash with Butter and Rosemary (page 144) and Carrot and Potato Purée (page 134), features the best of spring's produce.

Racks of Lamb with Port and Sultana Sauce   *Serves 4*

2 racks of lamb (8 chops each)
salt
pepper
1 cup port
½ cup chicken stock
1 bay leaf
3 tablespoons sultanas
2 cloves garlic
2 teaspoons cornflour
a little water

The sweetness of the lamb is emphasised with the port and sultana sauce. You only need a little sauce on the meat and it is delicious. If you prefer to reduce the sweetness add a little less port.

- Remove any excess fat from the lamb and wrap a piece of foil around the bones to prevent charring.

- Place the lamb, fat side down, in a dry frying pan and cook until the meat has changed colour. Remove the lamb from the pan, season, and place in a shallow baking dish or casserole dish in which it will fit fairly snugly.

- Wipe out the pan, pour in the port and stock, and add the bay leaf, sultanas and garlic. Bring to the boil and pour over and around the lamb.

- Preheat the oven to 180°C. Bake the lamb for about 25 minutes or until the meat is cooked.

- Carefully pour the liquid from the lamb into a saucepan. Mix the cornflour with a little water and add to the pan and cook, stirring, until the sauce is lightly glazed.

- Cut the lamb into chops and serve the sauce around them.

NOTE If you have trimmed the meat well the sauce should not be too fatty but if you are concerned you can skim any excess fat from the top before serving.

Lamb with Curried Apricot Glaze

Serves 4

4 racks of lamb (4 chops each)
10 dried apricot halves
⅓ cup water
1 cup orange juice
1 strip lemon rind
1 tablespoon brown sugar
1 tablespoon chopped shallot
2 tablespoons light olive oil
1 tablespoon curry powder
salt
pepper

The curried glaze can be quite spiced and hot, as you will only taste a little on the edge of each lamb chop. If the racks are large it may be best to cook them first for 10 minutes and then glaze so the topping does not caramelise and burn.

- Remove any excess fat from the lamb and wrap a piece of foil around the bones to prevent charring.

- Put the apricot halves, water, orange juice, lemon peel and brown sugar into a saucepan and cook for a couple of minutes or until the fruit has softened.

- While the apricot mixture is cooking, sauté the shallot in the oil until softened, add the curry powder and leave to fry gently.

- Put the apricot mixture into a blender or food processor and blend until smooth.

- Add the blended apricot mixture to the pan with the shallot and curry, and bring to the boil. It should be thick enough to brush on the meat. Season.

- Brush some of the mixture on the top of the racks of lamb. Place the racks in a baking dish and glaze, side upwards, with any leftover mixture.

- Preheat the oven to 180°C. Cook the racks for about 20 to 25 minutes, according to their size. During the cooking time glaze again with the apricot mixture. Reserve any leftover mixture.

- Remove the lamb from the oven and leave to rest for a couple of minutes. If you have leftover glaze, thin with a little chicken stock or water and use as a sauce to brush on the meat just before serving.

- Serve the racks whole or carefully cut into chops and arrange on a plate.

Lamb Fillets with Garlic and Tomato Sauce   *Serves 4*

8 cloves garlic, unpeeled
1 tablespoon light olive oil *or*
  peanut oil
500 g lamb fillets
1 cup chicken stock *or* veal stock
1 large ripe tomato
½ teaspoon sugar
salt
pepper
a little finely chopped fresh parsley,
  chives *or* chervil

*Lamb fillets have become one of the popular cuts of meat —
they have no fat, and are quick cooking and easy to serve. The
garlic is simmered in water first so the flavour is gentle and
aromatic rather than strident, and it is mashed into the sauce.*

- Place the garlic in a saucepan and generously cover with
  water. Bring to the boil and simmer gently for about 20
  minutes or until the garlic has softened. Drain.

- Heat the oil in a frying pan and add the lamb fillets, just a
  few at a time. Cook, turning several times, until the fillets
  are browned evenly on the outside and cooked but pink
  inside. They only take a few minutes to cook. Transfer to a
  plate and put another plate on top to retain the moisture.
  Leave to rest for 5 minutes.

- Wipe out the pan, add the stock and bring to the boil.

- Dice the tomato very small, flicking out some of the seed as
  you do this, and add to the pan with the sugar, salt and
  pepper. Cook until reduced by about one-third.

- Remove the skin from the garlic (it will come away easily),
  mash with a fork on a plate and stir into the sauce. Let the
  sauce heat through and add the parsley, chive or chervil.

- If the meat is becoming cool you can put it into the sauce for
  a couple of minutes.

- Slice the meat on a diagonal and spoon a little sauce over
  the top.

Lamb Chops with Mushrooms and Parsley

Serves 4

8 thick lamb chops (preferably
  middle loin)
250 g mushrooms, finely sliced
30 g butter
salt
pepper

TOPPING
4 tablespoons finely chopped fresh
  parsley
1 large clove garlic, crushed
1½ cups breadcrumbs made from
  stale bread
salt
pepper
60 g butter

*You may have to order the chops from your butcher for this
dish as the standard, ready-cut chop is usually a bit thin. Thinly
cut chops will result in the lamb overcooking before the
topping is crisp.*

- Remove any excess fat from the chops and use a toothpick
  to hold the tail of the chop neatly in place.

- Heat a heavy-based frying pan, add the chops and cook in
  the dry pan until brown on both sides. Drain on kitchen
  paper and wipe out the pan.

- Add the mushroom, butter, salt and pepper to the pan and
  cook over a high heat until the mushroom has wilted. Leave
  to cool while preparing the Topping.

- Mix the parsley, garlic and breadcrumbs, and season well.

- Melt the butter and mix into the breadcrumbs. If too dry
  melt a little more butter.

- To assemble, put some mushroom on top of each chop,
  pressing down well.

- Put the breadcrumbs on top of the mushroom and press flat.
  Place the chops on a greased tray.

- Preheat the oven to 180°C. Bake the chops for about 15
  minutes or until they are just cooked but still pink on the
  bone. If the topping is soft place under the grill for a couple
  of minutes to crisp.

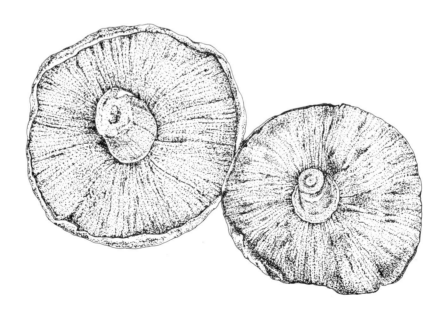

Leg of Lamb Maria

Serves 6–8

1 boned leg of lamb (about
  1.5–2 kg before boning)
pepper
1 tablespoon dry English mustard
2 tablespoons brown sugar
30 g butter
1 tablespoon redcurrant jelly
1 tablespoon lemon juice
¼ teaspoon ground cinnamon
1 tablespoon tomato sauce
a little water (if necessary)

The leg of lamb is boned and cut so it forms a flat butterfly shape, which reduces the cooking time considerably and makes the meat easy to carve and serve. The butcher will do this for you if you order it in advance. For some reason, which I can never quite fathom, a boned leg of lamb serves more people than an unboned leg.

- Preheat the oven to 200°C. Place the meat, fat side down, on the bench. Sprinkle pepper over the top of the meat, place in a baking dish and cook for about 20 minutes. Remove the meat from the oven and discard all the fat.

- While the meat is cooking, mix all the remaining ingredients in a small saucepan. Cook for a couple of minutes, stirring occasionally, until the redcurrant jelly has dissolved and the mixture is boiling.

- Return the meat, fat side down, to the baking dish. Spoon about half the sauce over the top and turn the oven down to 180°C. Cook for a further 15 minutes, then spoon the rest of the sauce on top and cook until the meat is ready. It should take about an extra 45 minutes. If the sauce on top of the meat begins to burn at any stage during the cooking, add a little water to check the caramelisation.

- Wrap the lamb in foil and leave to rest for 15 minutes. Cut into very thin slices and serve.

Gwenda's Fillet Steak with Caviar Sauce

Serves 4

4 thick pieces fillet steak
a little light olive oil

SAUCE
1 hard-boiled egg
2 teaspoons lemon juice
1 tablespoon finely chopped fresh
  parsley
2 tablespoons sour cream
1 teaspoon horseradish relish
1 tablespoon mayonnaise
60 g red caviar
salt
pepper

Hot steak with a cold sauce may seem unusual, but it makes an interesting dish, especially with the combination of meat and slightly salty caviar. Do not use the black lumpfish roe, as it discolours the sauce to an unpleasant murky grey: red lends a good colour. Of course, the better the caviar the better the sauce.

- Trim any fat or sinew from the outside of the steak.

- Brush the base of a frying pan with the oil. Heat the pan until it is smoking and add the steak. Cook over a high heat until brown on the outside and still pink inside – the time depends on the thickness of the steak.

- To make the Sauce, mash the egg with a fork and add all the remaining ingredients except the caviar. Only mix this in when you are ready to serve the dish. Season before serving (depending on the saltiness of the caviar).

- Serve the steaks on a warm plate. Put the caviar sauce in a bowl on the table or serve it in little individual dishes. Do not spoon the sauce over the meat when serving or the contrast of hot and cold will be lost.

Veal Chops with a Cheese Crust

Serves 4

4 veal chops
salt
pepper
45 g butter
1 cup dry white wine
1 small white onion
1 tablespoon grated Parmesan
  cheese
¼ cup grated St Claire *or* Jarlsberg
  cheese
¼ cup breadcrumbs made from
  stale bread
a little melted butter (if necessary)

Thick veal chops are much better than thin ones, and one per person should be sufficient if they are large. The cheese crust adds richness and gives a crunchy contrast to the lightness of the meat. The chops can be coated hours in advance and placed in the baking dish. Add the wine when you are ready to bake them.

- Season the chops with salt and pepper.

- Melt the butter in a frying pan, add the chops and cook on both sides until they have changed colour. Transfer to a shallow ovenproof dish in which they will fit in one layer without overlapping.

- Chop the onion and add to the same pan in which the chops were cooked. Stir until softened.

- Place the onion in a basin, add the two cheeses and breadcrumbs, and mix. If not moist add a little melted butter.

- With your hands, press a layer of this mixture on top of each chop, and pat it down firmly.

- Preheat the oven to 180°C. Pour the white wine around but not over the chops and bake for about 25 minutes or until the chops are tender and the topping is a crusty golden brown.

Veal Chops with Paprika and Onion Sauce

Serves 4

30 g butter
2 medium-sized white onions, cut
  into thin half-slices
1 clove garlic, finely chopped
1 tablespoon sweet paprika
¼ cup medium-dry sherry
½ cup sour cream
salt
pepper
4 veal chops (8 if small)
a little plain flour
2 tablespoons light olive oil

These veal chops have a sauce with a smooth, velvety pink richness similar to that usually served with Beef Stroganoff. Be sure to check you use sweet paprika rather than the hot variety, which would turn this tasty meal into a fiery dish.

- Melt the butter in a saucepan and add the onion. Cook until it has softened and is showing some tinges of gold.

- Add the garlic and paprika and fry for 1 minute.

- Pour in the sherry and sour cream, season, and bring to the boil. Cook gently for 2 minutes.

- Dust the chops with flour and shake away any excess.

- Heat the oil in a frying pan, brown the chops on both sides and transfer to a casserole dish with a tight-fitting lid.

- Preheat the oven to 180°C. Pour the sauce over the top of the chops, cover and bake for about 30 minutes or until the chops are very tender. If the sauce appears oily after cooking, stir the sauce when you serve the chops and the oiliness will not be so noticeable.

Veal in Curry Cream with Pears

Serves 4

4 thin veal schnitzels
a little seasoned plain flour
2 tablespoons light olive oil *or*
  peanut oil
30 g butter
1 firm ripe pear
2 teaspoons curry powder
1 cup dry white wine
½ cup thick cream
salt
¼ cup chopped macadamia nuts

Lightly curried pears spark up the delicate flavour of veal without overwhelming it.

- Dust the veal with the seasoned flour.

- Heat the oil in a large frying pan, add the veal and cook over a high heat until brown and tender, turning once. The veal should only take a couple of minutes on each side. Remove to a heated platter and keep warm. Wipe out the pan.

- Melt the butter in the pan in which the veal was cooked.

- Peel and core the pear and cut into small pieces. Add to the butter. Cook for 30 seconds, add the curry powder and fry for a few seconds.

- Pour in the wine, bring to the boil and add the cream.

- Cook until the sauce is lightly thickened, and season with salt.

- To serve, place the veal on serving plates, spoon a little sauce on top, dividing the pear as evenly as possible, and cover with some chopped nuts.

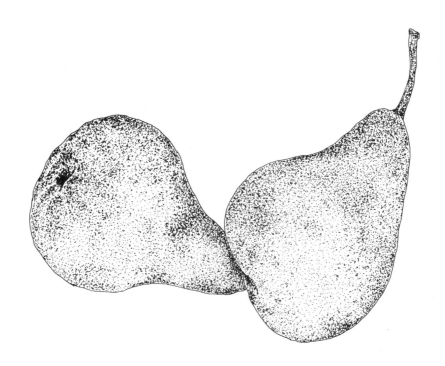

Chicken Breasts with Cashew Nut Sauce   *Serves 4*

4 chicken breasts, boned and
  skinned
1 cup breadcrumbs made from stale
  bread
½ cup sesame seeds
plain flour
1 large egg, beaten
3 tablespoons peanut oil
⅓ cup cashew nuts
1 tablespoon honey
1 tablespoon dark soy sauce
¾ cup chicken stock
pepper
30 g butter
3 tablespoons cornflour
a little water

This light easy dish is one of the most popular I ever serve. Do not use honey that is too rich and fragrant or it will overwhelm the chicken; if you do only have a flowery honey add a little less.

- With a wooden rolling pin flatten each chicken breast between plastic wrap so it is an even thickness.

- Mix the breadcrumbs and sesame seeds. Dip the chicken into the flour, then the egg and finally the breadcrumbs. Refrigerate.

- Heat 1 tablespoon of the oil and sauté the cashew nuts, stirring until golden. Drain on kitchen paper.

- Mix the honey with the soy sauce, stock and pepper in a basin.

- Heat the remaining oil and butter until foaming, add the chicken breasts and cook on both sides until golden brown. This should take 2 or 3 minutes on each side.

- Drain the chicken breasts on kitchen paper. Wipe out the pan and add the honey mixture. Bring to the boil.

- Mix the cornflour with a little water to make a thin paste, add to the pan and bring to the boil. The sauce will thicken almost immediately. Mix in the cashew nuts. Spoon a little over each chicken breast, distributing the nuts as evenly as possible.

Baked Quail with Bacon and Herbs   *Serves 4*

8 quail
8 sprigs parsley
8 sage leaves
8 cloves garlic, unpeeled
salt
pepper
45 g butter
8 rashers bacon, rind removed

Use fresh herbs with quail as the flavour is delicate; if you use dried herbs cut down the quantity considerably. Instead of using herbs and garlic in this recipe, an alternative is to tuck a wedge of orange, skin and all, into the cavity of the quail so the flesh will be lightly flavoured with citrus.

- Place into the body of each quail a sprig of parsley, a sage leaf and a whole clove of garlic.

- Season with salt and pepper inside.

- Melt the butter and brush over the birds.

- Wrap a rasher of bacon around the outside of each quail, ensuring you cover the breast, and secure with a toothpick.

- Preheat the oven to 180°C. Place the quail in a shallow metal baking dish and roast for about 25 minutes, turning them over once. The bacon will become crisp and the quail very aromatic and tender.

Baked Squab with Herbs

Serves 4

2 large *or* 4 small squab
a little light olive oil
salt
pepper
2 teaspoons freshly chopped thyme
2 teaspoons freshly chopped
  rosemary

Squab are baby pigeons that have not yet become airborne. They are generally about four weeks old and, as pigeons are devoted parents and lovers who mate for life, their breeding is expensive. The flesh is dark and compact with a slight gamey flavour and, as it is rich, a smallish serve is usually sufficient.

- Remove the wing tips from the squab and cut each bird into halves alongside the centre backbone. Place them on a baking tin, cut side down.

- Brush the top of the squab with a little oil and season with salt and pepper.

- Mix both herbs together and scatter over the top of the squab.

- Preheat the oven to 180°C. Bake the squab for about 20 to 30 minutes, depending on the size. While cooking, spoon any juices over the top.

- When ready, remove the squab from the oven, cover with foil and leave to rest for 10 minutes. Serve on hot plates, cut side down, with any juices from the pan spooned on top.

Golden Fish Fillets

Serves 6

6 large, thin fish fillets *or* 12 small,
  thin fish fillets
1/3 cup mayonnaise
1/3 cup whipped cream
1 tablespoon finely chopped fresh
  parsley
1 tablespoon French mustard
salt
pepper
lemon juice
lemon wedges for serving
a few sprigs parsley *or* a little
  watercress for garnishing

The topping will be sufficient to cover six large thin fish fillets such as whiting, or about ten small ones. You can make more as required. You do not need to thickly coat the fish; just a thin coating will do or the topping will dominate. Thin fillets are essential as they are grilled and not turned over so need to cook through fairly quickly.

- Pat the fish dry and check carefully there are no bones.

- Mix the mayonnaise, cream, chopped parsley, and mustard together and season with salt and pepper.

- When ready to cook, squeeze a little lemon juice on top of the fish, and preheat the grill. Brush oil on a flat tray that has sides. Place the fish fillets, skin side down if there is skin, on the tray.

- Spread a thin layer of the topping on each fish fillet and cook under the grill until the top is golden and bubbling. It should take only 4 to 5 minutes but depends on the fish and your grill.

- Serve immediately, lifting each fillet carefully from the tray with a spatula.

- Serve with lemon wedges and garnish with a few sprigs of parsley or a little watercress.

Fillets of Fish with Herb Topping

Serves 6

6 thin fish fillets
2 cloves garlic
5 tablespoons light olive oil
1 cup breadcrumbs made from stale
  bread
½ cup freshly chopped parsley
1 teaspoon freshly chopped
  marjoram *or* chives
salt
pepper
1 egg yolk

Thin fish fillets such as whiting are essential for this dish. They are baked and not turned over, so need to cook through fairly quickly. Aromatic with a speckled brown and green topping, the fillets make a beautiful first course and, doubled, an equally delicious main course.

- Pat the fish dry and check carefully there are no bones. Chop the garlic roughly and place in a small saucepan. Add the oil. Heat until the oil is very hot and remove from the stove. Leave to cool.

- Put the breadcrumbs with all the remaining ingredients, except the egg yolk, into a basin.

- Pour a sufficient quantity of the oil through a sieve into the breadcrumbs to make them moist. You may or may not need all the oil; it will depend on the type of breadcrumbs. They should just hold together lightly when pressed between your fingers.

- Beat the yolk in a small basin.

- Place the fish fillets, skin side down, onto some greased non-stick baking paper.

- Brush the top of each fillet with a little egg yolk.

- Place small handfuls of the breadcrumbs onto the fish. Some will spill over the sides but it is easy to pick them up. When you have formed a light coating press down very firmly with your hand to make as even a layer as possible.

- Preheat the oven to 180°C. Bake the fish for about 8 minutes for very thin fillets; 10 to 12 minutes for thicker fillets. Be careful not to over-cook. If after cooking the topping is not brown enough for your taste, a minute under the grill will crisp it immediately.

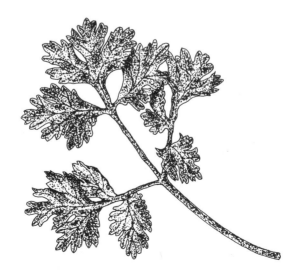

Prawns Cipriani

2 ripe tomatoes
boiling water
500 g shelled green prawns,
  deveined
seasoned plain flour
3 tablespoons olive oil
1 tablespoon capers
several slices sweet-sour cucumber
  or dill cucumber
60 g butter

Most tourists visiting Venice consider it almost obligatory to have a drink at the famous 'Harry's Bar'. Guiseppe Cipriani, who opened the bar, was one of the best known citizens of Venice and attracted a host of famous names during his lifetime. Somerset Maugham, Arturo Toscanini, Orson Welles, the Aga Khan, Barbara Hutton and the occasional king and queen have all sat at the bar. Another Cipriani creation is the famous and luxurious Cipriani Hotel on the island of Guidecca. One of the hotel's most famous dishes is Prawn Cipriani. In Venice it is served as a main course following a large plate of risotto or pasta; you can do the same or reverse the order and serve the prawns first.

- Place the tomatoes in a basin, pour boiling water over the top and leave to rest for 10 seconds. Peel them and cut into small dice.

- Dip the prawns into the seasoned flour and place in a colander. Shake gently to remove any excess flour.

- Heat the oil in a large frying pan. Add the prawns and cook, turning them over until they are pink on the outside.

- Chop the capers and dice the cucumber and mix both together.

- Put the tomato into the pan with the prawns and shake or stir gently for 30 seconds. Add the capers and cucumber and cook for 1 minute.

- Cut the butter into a few pieces, add to the pan, and let melt. Remove the pan from the heat so the butter does not continue cooking or it will make the sauce oily. Serve immediately.

NOTE If you can only buy unshelled green prawns, buy almost double the quantity.

DESSERTS

Iced Cherries

Serves 4

500 g cherries
water
ice cubes

This is more an idea than a recipe. You will find fruits served in this manner in both grand and tiny restaurants in Europe. The fruit is placed in a big bowl of iced water and presented by the waiter. A large slotted spoon is put alongside it so the water drains through as you pick out the fruit. The dish is perfect for cherries; their red skins glisten in the bowl and they are very crisp and juicy. The secret is not to leave them in the bowl for too long and, of course, the prettier the bowl the more effective the dish is. It is essential to buy the biggest, plumpest red cherries you can find.

- Discard any bruised cherries and leave the stalks on. If a slotted spoon is an impossible find, the cherries can be picked by the stalks from the bowl.

- Put a cup of water in a crystal bowl, add ice cubes so the dish is half full and rest the cherries on top. In about 20 minutes the ice will melt so the cherries will be just covered in chilled water.

- It is a good idea to put the crystal bowl on a platter so that drips do not go on the table.

Hot Spiced Cherries

Serves 4

¾ cup light dry red wine
½ cup sugar
½ cup water
1 stick cinnamon
3 thin strips orange rind, removed
  with a vegetable peeler
500 g dark cherries
1 tablespoon cornflour *or*
  arrowroot
2 tablespoons brandy

The secret of perfect hot cherries is to cook them so gently that they soften without wrinkling. They usually take only about 7 or 8 minutes. The wine and orange rind add an extra dimension of flavour, and the dish reheats very well.

- Put the wine, sugar, water, stick of cinnamon and orange strips into a saucepan and bring to the boil. Leave to cook gently for a couple of minutes.

- While the syrup is cooking remove the stalks from the cherries. Add the cherries to the hot syrup and cook, uncovered, until they have heated and are just soft.

- Mix the cornflour or arrowroot with the brandy and stir into the cherry sauce. It will thicken almost immediately.

- Serve warm with vanilla ice cream or simply on its own.

Lemon Mould with Cherries

Serves 4

1 × 450-g can cherries
3 teaspoons gelatine
2 tablespoons cold water
¾ cup castor sugar
grated rind of 1 lemon
2 tablespoons lemon juice
1 tablespoon brandy
1 cup unsweetened yoghurt
½ cup cream

This dessert is tart but has little of the sharp acid taste of yoghurt that many people dislike. It is meant to be made with unsweetened yoghurt and so the sugar has been added with this in mind. If you buy a sweet or vanilla-flavoured yoghurt you need to reduce the sugar. The dessert is refreshing and light and is a good finish for almost any main course.

- Drain the cherries (the juice is not used in the dish). Divide them evenly between four individual dessert dishes.

- Place the gelatine in a cup and mix with the cold water. Stand in a saucepan of hot water and leave to dissolve.

- Put the sugar, lemon rind, lemon juice and brandy in a basin. Stir with a fork to soften the sugar and then add the dissolved gelatine. Mix the yoghurt in with a fork.

- Whisk the cream until it holds soft peaks and fold through the yoghurt mixture.

- Pour the mixture over the cherries, cover the dishes and refrigerate for about 30 minutes to chill and set.

NOTE The dessert has 3 teaspoons of gelatine so it will set rapidly. If making a day in advance 2 teaspoons is sufficient.

Strawberries in Port

Serves 4

2 punnets (500 g) strawberries
2 tablespoons castor sugar
¼ cup port

This is a dish to try when you want to savour the first strawberries, which appear in spring. They are usually a little tart so the richness and sweetness of port adds perfume and flavour. This dessert is best served quite simply without any cream, which detracts rather than adds.

- Hull the strawberries.

- Place about a quarter of the strawberries on a dinner plate and scatter the sugar on top. Mash roughly with a fork.

- Place the mashed strawberries in a basin, add the port, and leave to marinate for about 1 hour.

- Put the remaining strawberries in a basin and when you are ready to serve pour the strawberry and port mixture over the top through a sieve. Press down to get the most flavour from the strawberries. They can be refrigerated for several hours but do not leave them too long or the berries will become soft.

Ice Cream with Coffee Sauce

Serves 4

½ cup cream
2 tablespoons instant espresso
  coffee
4 tablespoons crème de cacao
1 tablespoon brandy
vanilla ice cream
a little grated dark chocolate

This is a sophisticated version of the parfait you see in ice-cream shops, with its layers of ice cream, a spirit mixture and cream. Use parfait or wine glasses, but small ones because the dessert is very rich.

- Lightly whip the cream until it holds soft peaks.

- Place the coffee in a basin and add the crème de cacao and brandy. Stir to blend them together.

- Place a scoop of ice cream in the glasses, top with a small spoonful of cream, some of the coffee mixture, then another spoonful of ice cream, more cream and more coffee mixture and so on until the glass is full. Make the last layer cream.

- Top with the grated chocolate and serve immediately.

NOTE There should be sufficient sweetness in the ice cream but if you have a sweet tooth you can add 1 tablespoon of icing sugar to the espresso before mixing with crème de cacao and brandy.

Ice Cream with Rich Fudge Sauce

Serves 4

45 g unsalted butter
2 tablespoons brown sugar
2 tablespoons white sugar
1 tablespoon golden syrup
1 tablespoon cocoa
½ cup thick cream
1 teaspoon vanilla essence
vanilla ice cream
¼ cup unsalted, chopped
  macadamia nuts

The topping on this dessert is macadamia nuts; if you prefer, use walnuts, pecan nuts or blanched almonds.

- Melt the butter in a saucepan, add both types of sugar and cook, stirring, until the sugar has dissolved and the mixture is thick.

- Mix in the golden syrup and cocoa and stir well. Add the cream and simmer gently for about 3 to 5 minutes or until a thick sauce forms.

- Flavour with the vanilla essence.

- Place a scoop of vanilla ice cream into individual dessert dishes and pour the sauce over the top. Cover with the chopped macadamia nuts.

NOTE If you would like to toast the macadamia nuts you can either cook them in a shallow cake tin in the oven until golden or fry them in a dry pan until toasted. There is no need to toast walnuts or pecan nuts, but almonds can be browned.

Chocolate Coconut Torte

Serves 8

4 egg whites
1 cup castor sugar
1 cup desiccated coconut
3 tablespoons cocoa
½ teaspoon almond essence *or*
  vanilla essence

This torte has a crunchy topping and sticky moist middle. It can be served warm or cold and accompanied by ice cream or lightly whipped unsweetened cream. Any leftover torte keeps well for 24 hours. (See colour plate opposite.)

- Grease a shallow pie dish or round ovenproof dish.

- Beat the egg whites until they hold stiff peaks. Gradually add the sugar and continue beating for a couple of minutes.

- Place the coconut in a basin. Sift the cocoa over the top and discard any lumpy pieces in the seive.

- With a spatula, fold the cocoa mixture into the meringue, and flavour with the almond or vanilla essence.

- Preheat the oven to 180–190°C. Pour the mixture into the prepared dish, smooth the top and bake for about 20 minutes or until the top has set and it is crisp on the edges. The torte will firm as it cools and is best if not too hard.

- Cut into wedges and serve.

OPPOSITE PAGE ▶
Chocolate Coconut Torte topped with whipped cream and grated chocolate is an easy but effective dessert (this page).

Mixed Fruit in Maple Sauce

Serves 4

½ cup Canadian maple syrup
grated rind of 1 orange
½ cup orange juice
1 tablespoon lemon juice
2 large oranges
125 g fresh cherries
2 large bananas
1 tablespoon brandy
1 tablespoon Grand Marnier

If you can't get all three fruits – oranges, cherries and bananas – in season, use only oranges and bananas or substitute canned sweet cherries for the fresh ones. Strawberries can also replace the cherries, if desired. Buy a good Canadian maple syrup. (See colour plate opposite.)

- Put the maple syrup into a medium-sized saucepan with the orange rind, orange juice and lemon juice. Cook until it comes to the boil.

- Peel the oranges and remove the white pith. Cut into halves, place them, flat side down, on a board and cut into thin slices.

- Remove the cherry stalks.

- Cut the bananas into thick, chunky pieces.

- Place the orange slices and cherries in the syrup mixture and bring to the boil. Add the banana and cook for a couple of minutes or until softened.

- Add the brandy and Grand Marnier, warm, and serve before the fruit becomes too soft.

◄   *OPPOSITE PAGE*
Mixed Fruit in Maple Sauce combines fresh fruit, warming liqueurs and the mellow flavour of maple syrup to great effect (this page).

Glazed Kiwi Fruit

Serves 4

4 large kiwi fruit
⅓ cup apricot jam
4 large passionfruit
2 tablespoons brandy

Part of the charm of this fruit is its green, almost translucent, colour and when sliced it is shown to the best effect. Buy large kiwi fruit or allow 2 small ones per person, and prepare only an hour before serving or the flavour will be lost. This tart–sweet combination needs no cream and is best on its own.

- Peel the kiwi fruit and cut into slices. Arrange these overlapping slightly on small individual flat plates.

- Put the jam and the pulp of 2 passionfruit into a small saucepan. Heat until the jam is boiling and then push through a sieve.

- Mix in the pulp of the remaining passionfruit. Add the brandy, and cool slightly.

- Spoon a little of this mixture over the fruit on the plates, serving as evenly as possible.

- Refrigerate for 10 minutes before serving.

Quick Citrus Soufflé

Serves 4

15 g butter
a little sugar
4 eggs
1 extra egg white
½ cup castor sugar
grated rind of 1 large lemon
grated rind of 1 large orange
¼ cup lemon juice
1 extra tablespoon castor sugar
a little icing sugar

This soufflé is totally uncomplicated – just a mixture of egg yolks with lemon and orange rind and beaten egg whites. It has a fresh light flavour that can follow almost any dish. Be sure to beat the eggs yolks until very thick. Once cooked serve immediately as this style of soufflé will puff up beautifully but subside treacherously if kept for long.

- Grease a 5-cup capacity soufflé dish with the butter. Scatter with a little sugar and shake out any excess.

- Separate the eggs and add the extra egg white to the other four egg whites.

- Beat the yolks with the castor sugar until pale and very thick.

- Add the lemon and orange rind and lemon juice and mix through.

- Beat the whites until very stiff, add the extra tablespoon of castor sugar and beat again.

- Fold a third of the egg white mixture into the beaten egg yolk and then transfer this into the remaining egg white. Fold together.

- Preheat the oven to 180°C. Pour the mixture into the soufflé dish and bake for about 20 minutes or until the soufflé is puffed and golden. Leave the centre slightly creamy for the best flavour and texture.

- Sift the icing sugar over the top and serve instantly.

Oranges in Rosewater Syrup   *Serves 4*

4 large oranges
¾ cup freshly squeezed orange
  juice
2 tablespoons sugar
1 teaspoon orange flower water
1 teaspoon rosewater essence
a few rose petals for decorating

This is a perfumed dessert that has a refreshing quality and a lingering flavour.

- Remove wafer-thin strips of peel from two of the oranges and place in a saucepan, cover generously with water, and cook until softened. Drain.

- Return the peel to the saucepan, add the orange juice and sugar, and cook until the peel is transparent and the syrup glazed.

- Peel all the oranges of outside skin and pith. Cut the oranges into halves and then very thin slices, flicking out any pips. Place in a serving bowl.

- Remove the peel from the syrup and let the syrup cool. Add the orange flower water and rosewater essence and pour over the fruit. Refrigerate.

- Scatter the glazed peel on top of the fruit before serving.

- Decorate with a few rose petals.

Rhubarb Poached in Orange Syrup   *Serves 4*

grated rind of 1 large orange
¾ cup orange juice
½ cup water
1 stick cinnamon
1 cup sugar
500 g rhubarb, cut into 7.5-cm-long
  pieces

Springtime sees the early shoots of young rhubarb, which is tender, if rather astringent, but leaves a fresh, tart flavour. Poached in orange, rhubarb is a delight. If the rhubarb has any strings, gently pull them away before cutting into pieces.
Serve the dish plain or put a generous spoonful of cream in the centre of each bowl. It will gradually melt, forming a creamy thickening for the sauce. Although I love the dish warm, it can of course be eaten chilled.

- Place the orange rind and juice with the water, cinnamon and sugar in a saucepan and bring to the boil.

- Add the rhubarb and let it cook very gently, pushing the top pieces under the liquid as it softens. Do not place a lid on the pan or the rhubarb will cook to a mush rather than remaining in pieces. You need to keep the heat low.

- Once the rhubarb is just tender, remove from the heat and let it rest for about 5 to 10 minutes before serving.

- Remove the cinnamon stick and spoon the rhubarb into shallow bowls.

SUMMER

The preparation of meals seems easier in summer. These
sunny months are a time for great flexibility, and
entertaining becomes a joy when the atmosphere is informal
and there is such a wide range of fresh, colourful produce.
Salads can be as simple as sliced tomato trickled with a
good virgin olive oil and highlighted by fresh basil.
A good choice of fish is usually available as the waters are
calm, and stoned fruit are at their peak. Long hot days call
for spending as little time as possible in the kitchen:
barbecuing comes into its own, and stir-frying and sautéing
suit the style of summer.

FIRST COURSES

Eggs on a Bed of Capsicum Mayonnaise   *Serves 4*

1 large red capsicum
1 tablespoon lemon juice
½ cup mayonnaise
salt
pepper
a little light cream (if necessary)
6 hard-boiled eggs
12 small black olives (such as
  niçoise olives)

This dish could form the base for a simple version of antipasto, with its smoky-flavoured and pink-hued mayonnaise topped with circles of egg. A second dish could be slices of tomato with sprigs of basil and a trickle of virgin olive oil. The third dish could be thin slices of ham or a spicy salami. The whole effect would be of bright colours and robust flavours.

- Cut the capsicum into halves and remove the seeds. Flatten the halves and place, skin side up, on a grill tray.

- Cook the capsicum until the skin has blistered and is black. Remove and place in a paper bag. Leave for about 10 minutes to cool sufficiently for handling.

- Peel away the papery skin of the capsicum. Cut the flesh into rough pieces and place in a blender or food processor with the lemon juice. Blend to a pulp.

- Mix the capsicum pulp into the mayonnaise, and season. If too thick, thin with a little light cream.

- Put the capsicum mayonnaise onto an oval platter that is about 20 cm long and 8 cm wide.

- Cut the hard-boiled eggs into slices and arrange them in a single layer on top of the mayonnaise.

- Scatter with the olives and serve immediately.

NOTE You can make the capsicum mayonnaise a day in advance but, once sliced, the eggs should be served within the hour or they will begin to dry.

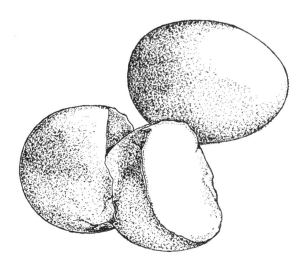

Cheese Toasts with Savoury Topping

Serves 4

4 thick slices brown *or* white bread
butter
125 g St Claire *or* Jarlsberg *or*
 Gruyère cheese

TOPPING
30 g butter
1 clove garlic, crushed
60 g ham, finely chopped
60 g canned pimentos, drained and
 chopped

The cheese toasts can make a tasty lunch dish or a snack or you can prepare small ones for a party and use them as an appetiser with drinks. The cheese is creamy and nutty, the topping rather smoky with the ham and pimento.

- Toast the bread and remove the crusts. Butter lightly.

- Cut slices from the cheese and place on top of the toast so it is completely covered to the edge. Preheat the oven to 180°C. Put the toast onto a flat tray and bake for about 6 minutes, or cook under the grill.

- To make the Topping, melt the butter, add the garlic, ham and pimento, and cook until heated.

- To serve, put a slice of toast on each plate and spoon the topping onto the centre.

Zucchini and Onion Salad

Serves 4

2 medium-sized onions
2 tablespoons virgin olive oil
250 g baby zucchini

DRESSING
4 tablespoons light olive oil
1 tablespoon white wine vinegar
1 teaspoon honey
1 teaspoon dry English mustard
salt
pepper

Cooking the onion gives a sweet flavour and makes the salad more interesting.

- Cut the onions into halves and then thin slices.

- Heat the oil in a frying pan, add the onion and cook until softened and tinged with gold.

- Cut the zucchini into fine slices or long strips and then into matchstick pieces.

- Add the softened onion to the zucchini, and mix.

- Mix all the Dressing ingredients together and stir through the salad. Taste and season. It needs plenty of seasoning as zucchini is a rather bland vegetable.

- Leave the salad to marinate for about 20 minutes but avoid leaving for too long, as the zucchini will eventually give out liquid, which makes the salad too wet.

Salad of Snow Peas with Melon and Ham   *Serves 4*

185 g snow peas
1 tablespoon light olive oil
45 g pine nuts
1 medium-sized canteloup
185 g ham cut into dice

DRESSING
6 tablespoons light olive oil
2 tablespoons white wine vinegar
salt
pepper
2 teaspoons honey

This is a bright, crunchy first-course dish that, because of its lightness, fits well into a menu that features a rich main course. The dressing has a little honey to give sweetness. Some of the varietal honeys are lovely but rather rich and perfumed, so be a little cautious with the kind you use.

- Bring a saucepan of salted water to the boil.

- Top and tail the snow peas and pull away the string as you do this. Add the snow peas to the pan and cook for a couple of minutes, depending on their size. Drain, refresh with a little cold water, and drain again. If preparing in advance, cover and refrigerate.

- Heat the oil in a frying pan. Cook the pine nuts until golden brown, stirring so they cook evenly. Drain on kitchen paper.

- Peel the canteloup, cut into halves, remove the seeds and cut the flesh into neat dice.

- Mix the ham with the canteloup and pine nuts.

- Mix all the Dressing ingredients together and whisk well. Taste and, if too sharp with vinegar, add more oil or adjust with honey.

- To assemble the salad, pour half the dressing over the canteloup mixture, stir gently, and leave to marinate for 10 minutes.

- Arrange a circle of snow peas on individual plates and fill the centre with the canteloup mixture.

- Moisten the peas with a small spoonful of the remaining dressing.

NOTE A more glamorous presentation is achieved by making canteloup balls using a melon baller, but you will need extra time and, as there is a lot of wastage, a large canteloup.

Prawns in Garlic Cream Sauce   *Serves 4*

500 g green prawns, shelled and
  deveined
45 g butter
2 cloves garlic, crushed
salt
pepper
½ cup cream
2 tablespoons finely chopped fresh
  parsley

A rich robust dish, garlic prawns can be as strong or mild as you like according to the quantity of garlic used. Too large a portion tends to be indigestible, so make the serves small and ensure the remainder of the meal is light in composition, especially dessert.

- Rinse the prawns and pat dry.

- Melt the butter in a frying pan, add the prawns and cook, turning, until they have changed colour. Add the garlic and fry for 30 seconds. Season with salt and pepper.

- Pour in the cream, bring to the boil, and simmer gently for about 30 seconds. Add the parsley and serve.

Smoked Salmon Spread

Serves 4

1 tablespoon onion juice
185 g smoked salmon
¾ cup sour cream
2 teaspoons horseradish relish
3 tablespoons mayonnaise
freshly ground black pepper

In the middle of the eighteenth century, salmon was smoked and sold as a delicacy in Russia, mainly to Jewish families. Later that century, one of the first commercial enterprises was founded in London. As it became well known the fish swept to popularity. It was a luxury then and still is, although with the advent of the Tasmanian salmon industry there is plenty of superb and often reasonably priced smoked salmon available. This spread can be served in small containers with triangles of toast alongside as a first course. (See colour plate opposite page 57.)

- Make the onion juice by grating an onion into a basin. Put through a sieve to get just the juice and none of the pieces of onion, which would be too dominating in the dish.

- Cut the salmon into very small pieces.

- Mix all the remaining ingredients together.

- Stir the smoked salmon through the mixture, place in four individual containers, cover, and refrigerate. The spread can be kept for 12 hours.

Tomatoes with Salmon Topping

Serves 4

4 ripe tomatoes
salt
pepper
a little sugar
1 × 220-g can red salmon
1 hard-boiled egg
2 tablespoons finely chopped onion
1 tablespoon finely chopped dill
 cucumber
1 small apple
1 tablespoon mayonnaise
1 tablespoon cream
finely chopped fresh chives *or*
 parsley for garnishing

This dish makes a pretty and light first course or lunch dish.

- Place the tomatoes in a basin and pour boiling water over them. Leave to stand for 10 seconds and then peel them. Cut the tomatoes into halves and if they do not balance trim a small piece from the base.

- Season the top of each one with salt, pepper and a small scattering of sugar.

- Remove the bones from the salmon and flake the fish.

- Mash the hard-boiled egg and mix with the onion and cucumber.

- Grate the apple and stir through the egg mixture. Add the mayonnaise, cream and salt to taste. This should be a well-seasoned topping.

- Place a mound of the topping on each tomato half, taking it neatly to the edge, and scatter the chives or parsley on top.

Scallops with Sweet Mustard Sauce

Serves 4

500 g scallops
seasoned plain flour
2 tablespoons light olive oil

MUSTARD SAUCE
2 teaspoons French mustard
1 teaspoon dry English mustard
2 teaspoons sugar
2 teaspoons white wine vinegar
¼ cup light olive *or* peanut oil
salt
pepper
1 tablespoon freshly chopped dill

The scallops are very simply cooked. The sauce, which is modelled on the mustard sauces served in Scandinavian countries with salmon lax, is served on the side for dipping.

- Trim any dark bits and the small piece of muscle from the scallops.

- Dust the scallops with the seasoned flour and leave for 5 minutes so the flour forms a coating.

- Heat the oil in a frying pan and cook the scallops, turning them over once, until they are lightly browned on the outside. Be careful not to over-cook them or they will be spoilt. Timing depends on their size. Transfer to kitchen paper to drain.

- To make the Mustard Sauce, mix the two mustards with the sugar and add the vinegar.

- Gradually whisk in the oil with a fork, taste, and adjust if required with more sugar or vinegar. Season with salt and pepper and stir in the dill.

NOTE The sauce can either be made at the last moment or well in advance. It will keep, covered and refrigerated, for about 2 days. Give it a good stir before using, as it may look separated, and then let it come back to room temperature.

Smoked Trout with Horseradish Cream

Serves 4

3 tablespoons mayonnaise
1 tablespoon horseradish relish *or* horseradish cream
2 teaspoons lemon juice
2 tablespoons lightly whipped cream
lettuce leaves
375–500 g smoked trout
1 medium-sized mild onion, finely chopped
a few capers

This is a classic and popular dish that makes an easy first course. Buy the best quality smoked trout you can get so it will be very moist. You can prepare it about 30 minutes in advance.

- Mix the mayonnaise with the horseradish relish, lemon juice and cream. Taste, and adjust to suit your own palate. Refrigerate. You can make this cream hours in advance.

- Put a piece of lettuce on each plate.

- Remove any skin and bones from the fish and arrange portions of the fish on the lettuce.

- Coat the top of the fish with the cream, scatter onion over the top and place a couple of capers in the centre.

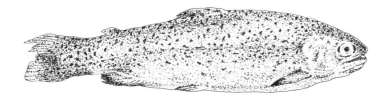

MAIN COURSES

Middle Eastern Inspired Slice

Serves 6

1 cup breadcrumbs made from stale
  bread
2 large eggs
½ cup milk
2 cloves garlic, finely chopped
2 teaspoons grated fresh ginger
a few drops Tabasco
500 g finely minced lamb
12 mint leaves, chopped

TOPPING
½ cup pine nuts
1 tablespoon oil
1 cup chopped frozen onion
½ cup yoghurt
2 eggs
1 tablespoon hot mango chutney

Make this in a quiche dish, preferably a china one so it can be served at the table. The casing is a layer of lamb and the filling a fresh-tasting, slightly spicy yoghurt mixture. It is delicious as a hot main course with salad or a cold picnic lunch. Be sure to order the lamb minced and low in fat, especially if the dish is to be eaten cold. You can also make this dish using minced beef.

- Grease a 20-cm quiche dish.

- Put all the ingredients, except the Topping ingredients, into a basin and beat using your hand with the fingers slightly open. The meat will become firm as everything blends together. Put into the quiche dish.

- Dampen your hands and smooth the top of the meat mixture. Wet the base of a dessertspoon and flatten the meat out on the bottom of the quiche dish. Press it up the sides so you have a shell. Level the edges with the back of the spoon so they are the same height as the quiche dish.

- Preheat the oven to 180°C. Bake the meat shell for about 15 minutes or until set. It will not be cooked through in the centre at this stage. Prepare the Topping while the meat shell is cooking.

- Place the pine nuts in a frying pan with the oil and cook, stirring, until golden. Drain on kitchen paper.

- Add the onion to the same pan and cook for a couple of minutes or until soft and pale golden. Transfer to a basin.

- Stir the yoghurt, eggs and mango chutney into the basin.

- When the meat shell is ready, if there is any liquid in the cavity either tilt carefully to remove or dab with kitchen paper.

- Pour the topping into the centre and scatter the pine nuts on top.

- Return the slice to the oven and cook for about 15 to 20 minutes or until the yoghurt has set.

- When cooked, leave the slice to rest for 5 minutes before cutting into wedges.

Racks of Lamb with Spiced Tomato Sauce   *Serves 4*

4 racks of lamb (4 chops each)
salt
pepper
1 large clove garlic

SAUCE
500 g ripe tomatoes
1 onion, finely chopped
1 large clove garlic, finely chopped
6 black peppercorns
¼ teaspoon salt
1 dried chilli *or* a little Tabasco
2 tablespoons white wine vinegar
2 tablespoons sugar
a little water *or* chicken stock (if
  necessary)

This very flavoursome tomato sauce is spiced with a little chilli. It goes well with a rack of lamb and is equally good with thick, grilled lamb chops.

- Remove excess fat from the lamb and with a sharp knife score the top of the rack in a diamond pattern.

- Cut slits between the bones, and season the lamb.

- Peel the garlic and cut into slivers. Insert a sliver in each of the slits between the bones.

- Wrap a piece of foil around the bones to prevent charring.

- To make the Sauce, cut the tomatoes into dice.

- Place the tomato in a saucepan with the onion and garlic, and cook over a low heat for 5 minutes or until the juices run.

- Add all the remaining ingredients and continue cooking for about 20 minutes or until quite soft.

- Press through a sieve to get out all the juices. If too thick you can add a little water or chicken stock. Leave aside.

- Preheat the oven to 190°C. Place the meat directly on the oven rack and a tray underneath to catch the fat. Cook for about 25 minutes, although the exact timing depends on the thickness and size of the rack. Once cooked, cover the lamb loosely with foil and leave to rest for 5 minutes.

- Warm the sauce.

- Serve the racks whole or cut into chops, resting on a puddle of the warmed sauce.

NOTE Cooking meat directly on the rack allows for even heat circulation and is a very good method for racks of lamb.

Lamb Fillets with Fried Basil Leaves

Serves 4

4 large *or* 8 small lamb fillets
⅓ cup virgin olive oil
2 tablespoons finely chopped fresh
  parsley
1 teaspoon finely chopped fresh
  thyme
2 tablespoons shredded fresh basil
  leaves
2 cloves garlic, finely chopped *or*
  crushed
pepper
additional virgin olive oil
⅓ cup water
1 tomato, chopped
a little light olive oil
16 extra fresh basil leaves

We associate lamb and basil with spring. However, this is a dish that is equally good made a little later, when the weather is warm, the basil has a more intense flavour and the lamb fillets are not too small. Although it takes a few minutes to trim the fillets of any sinew, the lamb tastes better as it is not chewy.

- Pat the lamb dry and trim the meat.

- Mix the virgin olive oil with the herbs, garlic and pepper in a basin.

- Roll the lamb in the oil mixture.

- Heat an additional teaspoon or two of virgin olive oil in a frying pan, add the lamb, and turn over until browned on both sides, keeping the heat very high. Turn the heat down and cook for a couple of minutes. Remove from the heat, take the lamb from the pan and leave to rest.

- Pour the water into the pan and stir to get up all the bits of herb and any brown specks.

- Add the tomato and stir until softened. Put a lid on the pan and let it cook over the lowest heat for a couple of minutes.

- Return the lamb to the pan and keep warm.

- Heat the light olive oil in a frying pan. When very hot, add the extra basil leaves (the oil will spit, so stand well clear). Cook until crisp. Be careful not to let the leaves brown or they become bitter. Remove with a slotted spoon to some kitchen paper, drain well.

- Cut the meat into slices, serve with a little sauce and arrange the fried basil leaves on top.

NOTE If you do not want to use fried basil, make the dish in exactly the same way but when serving shred some basil leaves very finely and scatter a few on top. You would need about 1 large leaf or 2 small leaves for each serve.

Leg of Lamb Trader Vic

Serves 6–8

1 boned leg of lamb, cut into a flat
  butterfly shape (about 1.5–2 kg
  before boning)
salt
pepper
2 onions, finely chopped
2 cloves garlic, chopped
2 tablespoons peanut satay paste *or*
  sauce
¼ cup lemon juice
2 tablespoons honey
a little water (if necessary)

*Famous for Polynesian and Asian food and exotic drinks with
extraordinary names, the Trader Vic restaurants are spread
across the United States. Chinese ovens, fed by branches of
burning bay oak, are used in the restaurants to cook marinated
pieces of meat, which are among the most popular of their
dishes. Spiced with satay paste or sauce, lemon and honey, this
dish was inspired by some of the food prepared at Trader Vics.
The best accompaniment is aromatic rice.*

- Place a skewer through the meat so it remains flat while
  cooking. Season with salt and pepper and place, fat side up,
  in a baking dish.

- Preheat the oven to 180°C. Cook the lamb for about 20
  minutes.

- Mix the onion with the garlic, add the peanut satay paste or
  sauce, lemon juice and honey, and stir.

- Remove the lamb from the dish and discard any fat in the
  dish. Turn the meat over so the fat side is down and pour the
  mixture over the top of the meat. Return to the oven and
  cook, basting every so often, for a further 35 to 40 minutes
  or until the meat is pink. If the sauce begins to caramelise in
  the dish add a little water.

- Remove the dish from the oven and cover with foil. Leave to
  rest for 15 minutes before cutting into thin slices. Spoon a
  little of the sauce over each serving.

Fish in Mango Sauce

Serves 4

8 × 60-g fish fillets (such as
  whiting)
½ cup seasoned plain flour
60 g butter

SAUCE
1 cup dry white wine
½ cup cream
1 medium-sized mango, chopped *or*
  sliced

*Fillets of fish are best for this dish rather than whole fish and
any fine-textured variety can be used.*

- Remove any fins from the fish.

- Dip the fillets into the seasoned flour and shake off any
  excess.

- Heat the butter in a large frying pan (you may need to use
  two if the pans you have are small). Add the fillets when the
  butter is foaming and cook very gently, turning over once.
  Transfer to a warm plate, cover with another plate to retain
  the heat and keep the fish moist, and wipe out the pan.

- To make the Sauce, pour the wine and cream into the frying
  pan and cook over a high heat.

- When the mixture has reduced by about a third, add the
  mango and cook for 1 minute or until the mango has
  softened, but do not let it cook to a pulp.

- Place the fillets on a platter with a small spoonful of the
  sauce on top of each one.

Fish Fillets in Orange Cream Sauce

Serves 4

4 × 155-g fillets of fish
salt
pepper
1 cup freshly squeezed orange juice
½ cup medium-dry sherry
½ cup thick cream
1 orange

As the flavour of this sauce is quite rich you can use a fish that is either strong or bland – the former will cope with the orange well while the latter will be lifted by the sauce's freshness.

- Remove any fins from the fillets and season the fish with salt and pepper.

- Pour the orange juice and sherry into a frying pan and bring to the boil. Cook for 1 minute and then add the fillets.

- Simmer very gently, just letting the liquid bubble on the edges, until the fillets are cooked on one side. Turn them over and cook on the other side.

- Transfer to a warm plate and put another one on top to keep in the heat and retain the moisture.

- Turn the heat up under the orange and sherry, add the cream and cook until the liquid has thickened.

- Peel the orange, removing all the pith. Separate the segments, place in the liquid and leave for 30 seconds to warm through.

- Place the fillets on plates and spoon just the smallest quantity of sauce on each one, dividing the orange segments equally between serves.

Fish Fillets with Parsley Crumb Coating

Serves 4

4 × 155-g fish fillets
salt
pepper
1 egg
2 teaspoon oil
1 cup breadcrumbs made from stale
  bread
⅓ cup finely chopped fresh parsley
½ cup vegetable oil *or* light olive
  oil
lemon wedges for serving

Breadcrumbs are a fairly commonplace coating for fish because they keep the fish moist and add an interesting crunchy texture. For more variation, herbs can be added to the coating, which gives additional flavour as well as an attractive speckled-green appearance. Any fish can be coated in this manner; just be sure it is filleted and well scaled.

- Pat the fish dry and season with salt and pepper.

- Beat the egg and oil.

- Mix the breadcrumbs with the parsley.

- Dip the fish into the egg and oil mixture to coat both sides and then hold for a moment to let the excess drip away. Then dip the fish into the breadcrumbs, patting them onto both sides gently to make an even, firm coating. Refrigerate if not cooking immediately.

- Heat the ½ cup of vegetable oil in a frying pan, add the fish and cook over a moderate heat on both sides until crisp on the outside and cooked through in the centre.

- Drain on kitchen paper and serve immediately, accompanied by lemon wedges.

Chinese-style Fish

Serves 4

4 small fish (about 250 g each)
juice of 1 large lemon
3 thick slices fresh ginger
⅓ cup chopped spring onion
3 tablespoons peanut oil
2 tablespoons soy sauce
1 teaspoon chilli sauce
pepper (optional)

This is a simple method of cooking small whole fish – snapper or bream or red mullet is ideal. The fish are served individually with the sizzling ginger and onion sauce on top. The younger the ginger, the better the flavour. (See colour plate opposite.)

- Make 2 diagonal slashes in the top of each fish through the thickest part to ensure even cooking. Squeeze some lemon juice over both sides of each fish.

- Line the grill tray with some foil so it will be easy to clean, and preheat the grill.

- Cook the fish on one side until the slashes have opened slightly and the fish is cooked, turn over, and cook on the other side.

- Cut the ginger into very fine slivers the size of matches, and mix with the spring onion.

- When the fish is almost ready, heat the oil in a frying pan. Add the ginger and spring onion, and cook over a high heat for about 30 seconds. Remove, add the soy and chilli sauces and shake or stir to mix.

- Put the fish on individual plates, pour a little of the sauce on top and serve immediately. Do not add salt, but you can season with a little pepper if you wish.

OPPOSITE PAGE ▶

Chinese-style Fish (this page) served on a bed of Bean Shoots with Ginger (page 130) is a light and refreshing summer dish.

Golden Chicken

Serves 4

2 medium-sized chickens
a little light olive oil
⅓ cup honey
2 teaspoons curry powder
2 tablespoons French mustard
1 teaspoon dry Keen's mustard

I was given this recipe from The Flying Nun, a restaurant in Texas, which featured this tasty dish on its menu. It was so popular it became the house speciality. A sauce is grilled on top of the chicken to make a deep, sticky golden-brown layer. Although I usually cook the chicken first, it can be prepared using a ready-cooked chicken. This is a dish for those with good appetites! (See colour plate opposite.)

- Cut the chickens down the backbone and place them on the bench. Flatten with your hands and brush the top with oil. Place in a baking dish.

- Preheat the oven to 180°C. Bake the chicken for about 45 minutes or until cooked through.

- While the chicken is cooking, mix the honey with the curry powder and both types of mustard.

- Remove the chicken from the oven, leave in the same dish and turn on the grill.

- Spread a layer of the honey mixture over the top of the chicken. It will melt and run over the skin easily. Put under the grill and leave until well coloured. Be careful not to leave it too long, as the honey burns easily.

NOTE If using a ready-cooked chicken you need to warm the chicken first and then cut it into portions or halves. Brush with the mixture and then carefully grill.

◄   *OPPOSITE PAGE*
Served here with crispy Baked Potato Slices (page 139), Broccoli with Almonds and Pimento (page 132) and roasted cloves of garlic, Golden Chicken is a succulent dish with a sticky, full-flavoured sauce (this page).

Chicken and Corn Pie

Serves 4

375 g minced chicken
2 tablespoons oil
1 onion, finely chopped
1 small red capsicum, finely
  chopped *or* cut into strips
1 cup breadcrumbs made from stale
  bread
2 teaspoons freshly chopped thyme
1 × 450-g can creamed corn
3 large eggs
1 teaspoon salt
plenty of freshly ground black
  pepper
60 g butter
6 sheets filo pastry

The casing is made of filo so is as light as a feather, and the filling of chicken and vegetables has the slight sweetness that corn gives a dish. Poultry shops often sell minced chicken. If minced chicken is unobtainable you can buy boned, skinned chicken breast and mince it in a blender or food processor. This pie can also be served as a first course, when it will feed eight.

- Put the minced chicken into a bowl.

- Heat the oil in a saucepan and add the onion and capsicum. Cook, occasionally stirring, until softened. Let the vegetables cool for 5 minutes.

- Mix the cooked vegetables into the chicken with the breadcrumbs, thyme, corn and eggs. Season well.

- Melt the butter.

- Put a sheet of filo in a greased shallow pie dish and brush with some of the melted butter. Put another sheet of filo on top, letting it extend over the edge of the pie dish. Brush with butter. Slightly overlap another sheeet and let it extend over the edge of the pie dish. Brush with butter. Continue until you have used 6 sheets of filo altogether, covering the base of the pie dish with layers extending out all the way round.

- Place the chicken filling in the pie dish, and one by one fold the sheets over the top. You will find they are rather creased but this makes a soft and pretty effect.

- Crunch any leftover filo at the top of the pie into a ball so it looks like a rosette and dab with butter (you may have to melt more).

- Preheat the oven to 180°C. Bake the pie for 30 to 35 minutes or until it is a deep golden brown. Leave to rest for 5 minutes.

- Tilt the dish and the pie will slide out casily onto a large plate or board, where it can be cut into big wedges for serving.

Split Chicken with Mustard Coating

Serves 4

1 × 1.5-kg chicken
salt
pepper
1 tablespoon light olive oil
1 tablespoon dry English mustard
1 tablespoon French mustard
2 teaspoons sugar
1 egg yolk
breadcrumbs made from stale bread

In Scandinavia a special mustard coating is used on Christmas ham. Mixed with egg, it sets into a spicy coating over the meat. The mustard coating in this recipe is similar but is used on chicken. It adds flavour and keeps it moist and succulent. Serve the dish hot or at room temperature but not chilled.

- Remove the wing tip from the chicken, cut alongside the backbone and spread out, pressing down firmly to flatten the chicken. Remove any fat and place in a baking dish. Season with salt and pepper and brush with oil.

- Preheat the oven to 180°C. Cook the chicken for only about 30 minutes or until the top is pale golden.

- Mix both mustards in a basin with the sugar and egg yolk.

- Spread the mustard mixture over the top of the partly cooked chicken and press the breadcrumbs gently on top. Some may fall into the dish but this is not important.

- Return the chicken to the oven and continue cooking for a further 20 minutes or until the chicken is cooked through and the breadcrumbs are slightly crisp.

- Cut the chicken into four for serving.

Chicken and Bean Shoots in Peanut Sauce

Serves 4

2 chicken breasts, boned and
  skinned
2 tablespoons peanut oil
2 onions, cut into thin half-slices
2 medium-sized carrots, cut into
  slices *or* matchstick pieces
1/3 cup water
250 g bean shoots, rinsed
2–3 tablespoons peanut satay sauce

A number of peanut satay sauces are commercially available. They range from mild to very hot and can vary in quality and thickness. Buy one that you like in flavour. The sauce can be thinned easily if too dense. This is a dish that makes a small amount of chicken stretch considerably.

- Cut the chicken breasts into thin strips.

- Heat the oil in a wok or deep frying pan and add the chicken. Cook until it has changed colour and is almost cooked. Remove to a plate.

- Add the onion and carrot to the wok, toss for a few minutes, add the water and cook for a further 2 minutes or until slightly softened. All the water should evaporate.

- Add the bean shoots and the chicken, and toss quickly.

- Mix the peanut satay sauce with sufficient water to give it the consistency of cream, pour over the vegetables and chicken, and toss for a minute. The chicken strips should be cooked through and the vegetables softened but retaining some texture.

Chicken Patties Scented with Thyme

Serves 4

½ cup breadcrumbs made from
  stale bread
1 large egg
500 g minced chicken
1 teaspoon salt
pepper
45 g softened butter
1 tablespoon thyme leaves
1 tablespoon light olive oil

SAUCE
250 g cherry tomatoes
1 teaspoon sugar
salt
pepper
dash of Tabasco *or* chilli sauce

Poultry shops will often sell minced chicken, which makes these patties very easy and quick to make. If minced chicken is unobtainable you can buy boned, skinned chicken breast and mince it in a blender or food processor. The centre of the patties is filled with a buttery thyme mixture that melts as they cook. The result is moist, succulent little patties.

- Place the breadcrumbs in a basin and add the egg and chicken. Season and mix well with your hands.

- Mash the butter on a plate, add the thyme leaves and mix well.

- Divide the chicken into eight portions. With damp hands flatten one portion out. Place a small piece of the thyme butter in the centre and fold the meat around. Form into a round patty and flatten. Continue with all the patties and refrigerate.

- Heat the oil in a large frying pan, add the patties and cook gently until lightly coloured on the outside and cooked through. Transfer to a warm plate and cover with a second plate to keep them moist.

- To make the Sauce, cut the cherry tomatoes into halves and tip into the frying pan in which the chicken was cooked.

- Toss over a high heat, seasoning with sugar, salt, pepper and Tabasco or chilli sauce. The tomatoes will soften in a couple of minutes.

- To serve, spoon a little of the sauce on each plate and place two patties on top.

Teriyaki Hamburgers

Serves 4

1 large clove garlic, crushed
1 small white onion, finely chopped
1 teaspoon grated fresh ginger
¼ cup dark soy sauce
1 tablespoon sugar
2 tablespoons dry sherry
500 g finely minced beef
1 tablespoon oil
½ cup water

It may be their national dish but the Americans did not invent the hamburger; it was a popular dish in Germany centuries before it was heard of in the United States. However, the Americans were the first to place the meat in a bun, enabling it to be eaten with your hands. A hamburger can be a very simple dish or as elaborate as you wish, with onions, spices, wine, capers, anchovies and the like added to minced meat – not, I hasten to add, all together.

The teriyaki hamburger seasonings in this recipe are popular on the Hawaiian islands. The hamburgers are highly flavoured and very juicy and moist. In summer they can, of course, be cooked on a barbecue.

- Mix the garlic, onion, ginger, soy sauce, sugar and sherry in a basin.

- Place the meat in another basin and add half the garlic mixture to the meat. Work it through with your hands. Leave to marinate for about 5 minutes.

- Form into four round patties and flatten them slightly.

- Heat the oil in a frying pan, add the patties and cook until browned on the outside. Leave them just slightly pink in the centre. The longer the hamburgers are cooked the drier they become.

- Transfer the hamburgers to a warm plate.

- Mix the water into the other half of the garlic mixture.

- Wipe out the frying pan, add the garlic sauce and bring to the boil. Cook for 1 minute or until lightly glazed. Serve a spoonful on top of each hamburger.

NOTE There is no salt in this recipe as the soy sauce adds a salty taste but if you use a light, not dark, soy sauce you may wish to season with a little salt. You can also add pepper if you wish or adjust the seasonings in the sauce that is spooned on the hamburgers.

Fillet with Peppercorn and Pimento Sauce   *Serves 6*

6 pieces fillet steak
½ cup dry white wine
2 tablespoons brandy
3 tablespoons port
½ cup thick cream
1 cup chicken stock *or* veal stock *or* beef stock
2 tablespoons canned pimentos, drained and chopped
2 tablespoons green peppercorns, drained
1 tablespoon light olive oil
salt

During the early 1970s two great chefs visited Australia. One was Paul Bocuse and the other was Michel Guérard. Their visit was particularly noteworthy because it was the first time two chefs with such reputations had travelled so far. While here they created a menu with a main course of local duck coated with a peppercorn and pimento sauce, and they let me watch them in the kitchen as they prepared it.

This recipe uses a short-cut version of the sauce. It teams superbly with a sautéd breast of duck but I enjoy it as much with a fillet steak.

- Trim the steak and press down to flatten slightly.

- Put the wine, brandy and port into a saucepan and bring to the boil. Cook until it has reduced by one-third.

- Add the cream and stock, and cook until it has reduced by one-third and lightly thickened.

- Add the pimento and peppercorns, and leave aside until the steaks are ready.

- Heat the oil in a frying pan and when it is smoking hot add the steaks and cook on both sides until crusty brown on the outside and pink inside.

- Taste the sauce, as it may or may not need salt according to the stock. Pour a little sauce on top of each steak when serving.

Rice with Prawns

Serves 4

750 g unshelled green prawns
5 cups water
1 teaspoon salt
1 onion, finely chopped
3 tablespoons virgin olive oil
2 cups long-grain rice
1 tablespoon tomato paste
3 tablespoons finely grated
 Parmesan cheese
45 g butter
extra grated Parmesan cheese for
 serving

You need unshelled green prawns for this dish so that a light stock can be made with the shells. It only takes a few minutes to shell them and make the stock, and it will make the difference between a rather ordinary-tasting rice dish and one that is full of the flavour of the sea.

- Shell the prawns. Place the shells in a saucepan, add the water and salt. Bring to the boil, partly cover, and cook gently for about 15 minutes. Drain, reserving the liquid, and discard the shells.

- Put the onion into a heavy-based saucepan with 2 tablespoons of the oil and fry for a couple of minutes.

- Add the rice and cook, stirring constantly, until some of the grains have become opaque.

- Measure 4 cups of stock. If you need more add water to make up the amount. Add the tomato paste to the stock. Pour the stock over the rice, bring to the boil, cover the pan, and turn to a low heat. Cook for about 15 minutes or until almost ready.

- While the rice is cooking, heat the remaining tablespoon of oil and lightly fry the prawns until they have changed colour. Cut them into quarters or halves, depending on their size.

- Push the prawns into the rice, tucking them under so they will cook in the warmth of the grain. Continue cooking for 5 minutes.

- Add the butter and leave to melt. Scatter the Parmesan cheese on top and lightly fork the rice to separate the grains.

- Serve with some more grated Parmesan cheese on the table.

Scallops with Mushrooms and Peppercorns   *Serves 4*

750 g scallops
1 cup dry white wine
1 cup water
salt
pepper
375 g small mushrooms
30 g butter
½ cup cream
1 tablespoon pink peppercorns,
  rinsed and drained

Pink peppercorns are pickled in a jar and should be rinsed well so the vinegar taste is removed. They are spicy but not hot and give an interesting crunchy taste to the scallops.

- Trim any dark bits and the small piece of muscle from the scallops.

- Place the wine, water and salt and pepper in a saucepan, and simmer gently for about 3 minutes.

- Add the scallops and heat but do not boil. After they are plumped up, which usually takes 1 minute, transfer with a slotted spoon to a bowl or a plate, and place a plate on top to keep the scallops moist. Reserve the cooking liquid.

- Cut the mushrooms into halves unless they are very small. Melt the butter in a large frying pan. When foaming add the mushroom and cook over a high heat for 1 minute. Pour 1 cup of the liquid from the scallops over the top, and cook over a very high heat until it has almost reduced to a syrup. Add the cream and cook until thick.

- Return the scallops to the pan and warm gently, stirring through the peppercorns.

Tuna with Sesame Soy Sauce   *Serves 4*

4 × 150-g tuna steaks
1 tablespoon sesame seeds
3 tablespoons oil
2 tablespoons soy sauce
2 teaspoons sugar
1 teaspoon grated *or* shredded fresh
  ginger
2 tablespoons water
1 spring onion, cut into thin
  diagonal slices
a little lemon juice

The secret to serving moist, not dry, tuna is to just barely cook it. Like a steak, this particular fish is best left pink in the centre.

- Using the palm of your hand flatten the tuna steaks a little so they are thin.

- Place the sesame seeds in a dry frying pan. Cook, stirring with a fork, until golden and then transfer to a basin.

- Add 2 tablespoons of the oil, soy sauce, sugar, ginger and water to the basin.

- Heat the remaining 1 tablespoon of oil in the frying pan. Add the tuna steaks and cook over a high heat for about 1 minute on each side. They must be quite red in the centre. Transfer to a warm plate and put another one on top.

- Tip the sesame seed mixture into the pan and bring to the boil. Cook for about 30 seconds over a high heat until slightly reduced. Add the spring onion and a dash of lemon juice to taste.

- Arrange the tuna steaks on individual plates and spoon the sauce on top.

Ocean Trout on Wilted Salad Greens

Serves 4

250 g filleted tail end of ocean trout
  or Atlantic salmon
salt
freshly ground black pepper
⅓ cup light olive oil
3 teaspoons sugar
3 teaspoons Dijon *or* French
  mustard
1 tablespoon white wine vinegar
4 small handfuls mixed lettuce
3 tablespoons finely chopped *or*
  snipped fresh chives

For a long time a great favourite in a number of restaurants was a dish of hot fish placed on mixed greens and topped with a vinaigrette dressing. The warmth of the fish softened or wilted the greens and the dressing coated the fish and almost soaked into the flesh.

Delicious and savoury, the dish is ideal for fast and last-minute cooking. Pink-fleshed ocean trout or Atlantic salmon are the best types of fish to use. Buy the fish filleted, ready to slice, so the entire dish will only take a few minutes to assemble. When buying mixed lettuce, choose the mixed cress or a variety of lettuce known as mesclun.

Small servings go well before a meat dish, provided the meat is not too rich in flavour. Alternatively, the fish can be served as a very light main course or a perfect lunch dish for two.

- Put the filleted fish on a board and cut into about eight thinnish slices on a slight diagonal. If not using immediately cover with some plastic wrap and refrigerate.

- Season the fish with a little salt and plenty of freshly ground black pepper.

- Brush some of the oil over the base of a frying pan.

- Mix the remainder of the oil with the sugar, mustard and vinegar.

- Place a small handful of lettuce on four plates ready for the fish.

- Heat the pan and, when almost smoking, add the fish and cook for only about 30 seconds on each side, turning over as soon as one side has changed colour. Put two slices of fish on top of the lettuce on each plate.

- Off the heat (the mixture will splatter) add the oil and sugar mixture to the pan. Stir until you have picked up any brown bits from cooking the fish. Taste, and if too sweet add a dash more vinegar; if too sharp add a dash more sugar.

- Spoon the dressing over the fish and then put a little on the lettuce. Top the fish with a small scattering of chives. Serve instantly while the fish is hot and before the lettuce wilts too much.

DESSERTS

Apricots Filled with Amaretti Biscuit Cream   *Serves 4*

6 ripe apricots
juice of ½ lemon
½ cup cream
1 tablespoon icing sugar
1 tablespoon Marsala *or* sweet
  sherry
3 tablespoons Amaretti biscuit
  crumbs
2 teaspoons brandy
angelica for garnishing

Amaretti are little macaroons made from bitter almonds. You can buy them in supermarkets or delicatessens that sell imported biscuits. You can use sweet macaroons but the flavour is different and you need to use less sugar.

Prepare close to serving so the apricots will be very fresh and the cream will have little crunchy pieces in it. I have allowed three apricot halves per person but if the apricots are small allow four; if large, two apricot halves may be sufficient.

- Cut the apricots into halves, remove the stones, and brush the outside edge with lemon juice.

- Whip the cream until stiff. Add the icing sugar and Marsala and mix. Add the biscuit crumbs and brandy.

- Spoon the cream into the apricot halves and refrigerate for about 20 minutes.

- Put a little strip of angelica on top of each apricot half and serve.

Apricots with Streusel Topping   *Serves 4*

500 g ripe apricots
1 tablespoon castor sugar
1 tablespoon brandy

STREUSEL TOPPING
2 tablespoons brown sugar
1 tablespoon plain flour
45 g ground almonds
grated rind of 1 lemon
60 g butter

Other fruits, such as nectarines cut into halves, peaches cut into quarters, fresh cherries or deep-purple plums, can be used in this dish.

- Cut the apricots into halves and then into quarters and place in an ungreased shallow ovenproof dish in one layer.

- Preheat the oven to 180°C. Scatter the castor sugar on top of the apricot, add the brandy and cook for 6 minutes while preparing the Streusel Topping.

- Put the brown sugar, flour, almonds, and lemon rind into a basin and mix lightly.

- Cut the butter into small pieces and mix through the almond mixture until crumbly.

- Scatter the topping over the warm fruit and return to the oven. Cook for a further 20 minutes or until the apricot is soft and the topping coloured.

Canteloup with Rosewater Sauce

Serves 4

2 baby canteloups
1 punnet (250 g) raspberries
2 tablespoons castor sugar
1 teaspoon orange flower water
2 teaspoons rosewater essence
1 tablespoon brandy
grape leaves for serving

The perfume of raspberries and rosewater has a wonderful affinity with canteloup. Rosewater essence can be bought from shops that stock Oriental foods, and from the gourmet section of some supermarkets. Orange flower water can be found in health-food shops, some supermarkets and some chemists. The quality varies; the better it is the stronger. Adjust the quantity to suit your taste but do not use too much – a little rosewater gives a breath of sweetness, too much and the dessert will be cloyingly perfumed.

- Cut the canteloups into halves and remove the seeds. Refrigerate while preparing the sauce.

- Put the raspberries into a basin and add the remaining ingredients. Stir gently and leave at room temperature for about 10 minutes, then cover and refrigerate.

- Put a grape leaf on each plate. Put a canteloup half on top and fill the centre with the raspberry and rosewater sauce.

NOTE If you cannot buy baby canteloups choose one large one but present it differently. Cut into slices and arrange on individual plates in a fan shape and spoon the raspberry and rosewater sauce over the top.

Grapes in Honey Sauce

Serves 4

1 tablespoon honey
2 tablespoons brandy
1 teaspoon lemon juice
375 g seedless grapes, rinsed and
  stalks removed

Grapes prepared in this way can be eaten within a couple of hours but the sauce will be even better 24 hours later. Buy small sultana grapes. Rinse lightly, pull them away from the stalks and then leave to drain.

- Place the honey, brandy and lemon juice in a saucepan and warm gently until the honey has softened.

- Put the grapes into a bowl, pour the honey mixture over the top, and stir gently.

- Refrigerate until ready to serve.

Orange Sabayon

Serves 4

3 egg yolks
2 tablespoons castor sugar
2 tablespoons Grand Marnier
1 tablespoon brandy
2 punnets (500 g) strawberries *or* other fresh fruit

Serve the sabayon over any fresh fruits in season – strawberries are ideal, as are orange segments, kiwi fruit or slices of fresh ripe pear.

- Place a saucepan half-filled with water on to boil.

- Place the egg yolks, castor sugar, Grand Marnier and brandy in a china or glass basin that will fit in the saucepan. The water should be level with the mixture but no higher.

- Whisk for about 5 minutes or until the sauce becomes pale and fluffy.

- Remove the basin from the saucepan and continue beating for another minute so the sauce does not set on the sides or base of the basin.

- Hull the strawberries and arrange in individual dishes. Spoon the sauce over the top. You can either use it warm or at room temperature.

NOTE This sauce stays fluffy for a couple of hours if it is made properly. However, if it collapses just whip about ½ cup of cream and stir the sauce into it gradually. The sabayon will be different but you will still be able to use it.

Papaw with Passionfruit Sauce

Serves 4

750 g papaw
2 tablespoons lemon juice
3 tablespoons castor sugar
2 large passionfruit

The passionfruit sauce will add sweetness and freshness to any papaw, whether tasty and succulent or a little disappointing. The dessert will keep well in the refrigerator for 24 hours.

- Cut the papaw into halves and remove the seeds and skin. Cut into bite-sized pieces and place in a bowl.

- Mix the remaining ingredients and pour over the top of the papaw.

- Turn gently so the papaw is coated with the passionfruit sauce, and then refrigerate for at least 1 hour.

NOTE A dish such as this is best served on its own; cream seems to detract from the flavour.

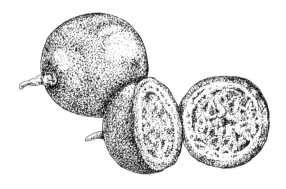

Peaches in the Style of Madame Point   *Serves 4*

1 punnet (250 g) strawberries
3 tablespoons icing sugar
2 tablespoons kirsch
3 tablespoons whipped cream
4 white peaches

A dessert of peaches with this name was created at the great French restaurant called 'La Pyramide'. The late Fernand Point, acknowledged as one of the greatest chefs in France, gradually developed the restaurant from a modest inn to one of the most important restaurants in Europe. He would have used perfect white peaches, sun-ripened strawberries and the slightly acidic cream of France. This is an exquisite dish but only when the fruits are at their peak of flavour.

- Hull the strawberries, chop them finely and push through a sieve or blend in a blender or food processor.
- Add the icing sugar and kirsch to the sieved strawberry, and mix.
- Fold the strawberry mixture into the cream so it is evenly mixed. Refrigerate.
- When ready to serve, peel the peaches and cut into slices. If the peaches are large the slices can be a bit awkward to serve, so cut into dice.
- Spoon the strawberry mixture into shallow champagne glasses and arrange the peach slices so they float on top. Serve immediately.

Flaming Peaches   *Serves 4*

8 small peaches
½ cup sugar
1 cup water
¼ cup kirsch
2 tablespoons Grand Marnier

This is a simple but exquisite dish that does not need cream or ice cream served with it. Buy small ripe yellow or white peaches for the most attractive result. The dish can be cooked in advance and warmed again when ready to serve.

- Carefully peel the peaches.
- Heat the sugar with the water and add the peaches, spooning some syrup over the top so they keep their colour. Cook gently for about 6 minutes or until heated through.
- Add 1 tablespoon of the kirsch and all of the Grand Marnier to the peaches.
- Put the peaches on a shallow platter with an edge, and pour just a little syrup around them.
- Warm the remainder of the kirsch.
- Take the peaches to the table, light the kirsch and pour over the top. Because of the sugar in the peaches the liqueur will burn for some time.

Baked Pineapple with Rum   *Serves 4*

1 medium-sized pineapple
4 tablespoons brown sugar
1 teaspoon ground cinnamon
3 tablespoons brown rum

No matter how sweet and ripe the pineapple, be sure not to over-cook it as the sugar in the fruit rapidly changes to acid and produces a very sharp taste.

- Cut the pineapple into halves lengthwise, dividing it as carefully and evenly as possible so you get a little bit of the green top on each portion. Cut each one into quarters lengthwise.

- Wrap a piece of foil around the green top of each portion so it will not brown in the oven.

- Put the pineapple quarters, skin side down, onto a metal baking sheet and scatter the brown sugar and cinnamon on top.

- Preheat the oven to 180°C. Bake the pineapple for about 10 minutes or until the sugar has melted. Transfer to individual plates and remove the foil.

- Warm the rum in a small saucepan, light it, and pour a little over each pineapple quarter. The sugar on top will make it burn brilliantly.

NOTE As the pineapple is still attached to the skin you will need to set knives and forks to make this easy to eat. The pineapple can be cut out in sections, or the entire strip removed and the sections cut into slices quite easily, by each diner.

Pineapple and Strawberry Coronet   *Serves 6*

1 ripe pineapple
2 tablespoons castor sugar
2 tablespoons kirsch
1 punnet (250 g) strawberries
1/3 cup lightly whipped cream
2 teaspoons icing sugar
1 teaspoon orange flower water

This is a simple dessert that looks exotic because of its presentation. A large platter presents it to the best advantage. The flavours are very fresh.

- Cut the top and base from the pineapple and remove the skin.

- Cut the pineapple into halves lengthwise, remove the core, and cut into thin slices.

- Place the pineapple in a basin. Scatter the castor sugar on top, add the kirsch, and leave to marinate for about 20 minutes (it can be left for several hours).

- Hull the strawberries. Reserve one of the best and cut the rest into halves (if large). Place in a basin.

- Mix the cream with the icing sugar and orange flower water, and stir through the strawberries. Refrigerate.

- Mound the strawberries in the centre of a platter and arrange the pineapple slices overlapping in a circle around them. Spoon the juices from the pineapple over the top, and place the reserved strawberry on top of the centre mound.

Strawberry Syllabub

Serves 4

1 punnet (250 g) strawberries
½ cup castor sugar
2 tablespoons lemon juice
3 tablespoons dry white wine
1 tablespoon brandy
1 cup cream

This delicious creamy dessert can be served either in individual dishes or one large bowl, from which it is served out.

- Hull the strawberries and reserve a quarter of them. Purée the remainder.

- Mix the castor sugar with the lemon juice, wine and brandy.

- Whip the cream until it holds stiff peaks.

- Mix the strawberry purée into the sugar mixture and gradually add to the cream, whisking constantly. It will form soft mounds, lighter than whipped cream but firm enough to hold a shape. Refrigerate if not serving immediately. The syllabub keeps for about 6 hours.

- Divide the reserved strawberries between four bowls.

- Top the strawberries with the syllabub and refrigerate until ready to serve.

NOTE If stored in the refrigerator for more than 24 hours some liquid may seep to the base of the dish. The liquid does not affect the flavour, only the appearance.

Strawberries with Raspberry Sauce

Serves 4

2 punnets (500 g) strawberries
1 tablespoon castor sugar

SAUCE
1 punnet (250 g) raspberries
3 tablespoons icing sugar
1 tablespoon orange-flavoured
  liqueur
½ teaspoon vanilla essence
2 tablespoons lightly whipped
  cream

This dish combines the best of all summer flavours in one tart, fresh-tasting dessert.

- Hull the berries and place in a basin. Scatter with castor sugar and stir. Refrigerate.

- To make the Sauce, push the raspberries through a sieve into a basin, discard the seeds and add the icing sugar, liqueur, vanilla essence and cream. Stir well and refrigerate.

- To assemble, place the strawberries in individual dishes and pour a generous amount of sauce over the top.

NOTE If you have any leftover sauce use it on ice cream or cake, or with any plain vanilla pudding.

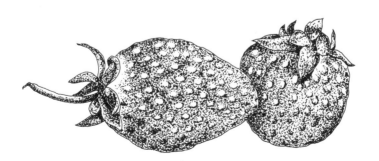

Baked Raspberry Pudding

Serves 4

1 punnet (250 g) raspberries
1 egg
½ cup castor sugar
½ teaspoon vanilla essence
1 tablespoon plain flour
30 g ground almonds
½ cup cream

Blackberries, loganberries or slices of ripe apricots or peaches can be used instead of the raspberries in this pudding, although the raspberries are best of all. (See colour plate opposite.)

- Place the raspberries in a shallow 20-cm × 10-cm ovenproof dish.

- Beat the egg, castor sugar and vanilla essence with a whisk until thick.

- Add the flour, almonds and cream to the egg mixture and mix. Pour as evenly as possible over the raspberries.

- Preheat the oven to 180°C. Bake the raspberries for about 20 minutes or until lightly set. The pudding should still be a little creamy in the centre. Leave to rest for 5 minutes before serving.

OPPOSITE PAGE ▶
Baked Raspberry Pudding features one of summer's most luscious berries (this page).

Strawberries with Banana Passionfruit Cream *Serves 4*

2 punnets (500 g) strawberries
2 medium-sized ripe bananas
3 tablespoons castor sugar
2 tablespoons orange-flavoured
  liqueur
pulp of 2 passionfruit
½ cup cream

Small strawberries can be left whole, larger ones are best halved. The banana passionfruit cream needs to be made close to serving time, as even with care the fresh flavour and colour deteriorate quickly.

- Hull the strawberries and place in four individual bowls.

- With a fork, mash the bananas on a dinner plate. Add the castor sugar. Stir with a fork until the sugar has softened.

- Transfer the banana to a bowl and add the liqueur and passionfruit pulp.

- Whisk the cream until it holds soft peaks and add the banana mixture. Spoon over the strawberries and refrigerate.

NOTE The dessert can be decorated with whole strawberries, in which case you need to reserve some; or you can spoon a little passionfruit pulp over the top. I have also made this dessert with mixed berries, using strawberries and raspberries for a change.

Strawberries with Lemon Cream *Serves 4*

2–3 punnets (500–750 g)
  strawberries
¾ cup sour cream
grated rind of large lemon
2 tablespoons lemon juice
3 tablespoons icing sugar

The lemon cream is used as a dip rather than being poured over the top of the strawberries. Use large strawberries for the easiest dipping. Other fruits, such as wedges of papaw, chunky pieces of canteloup or quarters of kiwi fruit, could be substituted.

- Do not hull the strawberries, and if you have to wash them just drop gently into a bowl of water and drain on kitchen paper. Refrigerate.

- Mix all the remaining ingredients. Taste, and if too sharp add more sugar; if too sweet add more lemon. Refrigerate.

- Serve the strawberries on individual plates with a small container of the lemon cream or make up a big platter on the table.

◄   *OPPOSITE PAGE*
Smoked Salmon Spread, served in individual dishes and accompanied by triangles of toast and crudités, makes a delicious, light first course (page 33).

Honey and Almond Sauce for Ice Cream   *Serves 4*

45 g unsalted butter
2 teaspoons cornflour
¾ cup honey
¼ cup freshly squeezed orange
  juice
3 tablespoons slivered almonds
vanilla ice cream

This is a perfumed and fragrant sticky sauce to be spooned over ice cream. The type of honey you use will determine the taste of the sauce; very sweet honey will create a very sweet sauce. It can be made in advance and refrigerated. If you put it in a narrow-necked jar you may have trouble spooning it out. Only use a little of this rich sauce as a topping, and a scattering of browned almond slivers is a good crunchy addition.

- Melt the butter and mix with the cornflour.

- Add the honey to the cornflour mixture and cook gently until the mixture has come to the boil.

- Add the orange juice to the saucepan, remove from the heat and stir. Leave aside until just warm.

- Put the almonds into a dry frying pan, toss until lightly coloured and leave aside.

- Place the ice cream in individual dishes, spoon the warm honey sauce on top and scatter with a few slivered almonds.

Quick Vanilla Ice Cream   *Serves 4*

3 eggs
½ cup sugar
1 tablespoon honey
1¼ cups cream
1 teaspoon vanilla essence

This beautifully creamy ice cream can be made without an ice-cream machine and keeps well for 5 days. As there is no cooking involved this dessert is very fast to prepare. However, remember to allow around 4 hours for the ice cream to freeze.

- Separate the eggs.

- Add the sugar and the honey to the yolks and beat until fluffy.

- Beat the cream until it holds soft peaks and mix with the vanilla essence into the yolk mixture.

- Carefully pour the yolk and cream mixture into a shallow metal tin and put into the freezer for about 1 hour or until firm.

- Beat the egg whites until stiff.

- Break up the yolk and cream mixture with a fork and beat until creamy.

- Fold the egg whites gently through the yolk and cream mixture.

- Carefully pour into a metal cake or log tin.

- Freeze until firm, then cover with plastic wrap.

AUTUMN

The food of autumn has a great deal to do with aromas
and associations: the earthy smell of mushrooms picked
from the fields, the crackling of papery leaves underfoot,
and soup bubbling away on the stove as a chill creeps into
the air. Early autumn gives us produce with
sun-ripened flavours: tomatoes, fleshy capsicums, eggplant
and berries. As the season progresses, a need for
rustic food sets in.

FIRST COURSES

Chicken Sausage and Sweet-potato Soup   *Serves 4*

500 g sweet potatoes (preferably
  kumara), peeled and roughly
  chopped
1 medium-sized potato, peeled and
  roughly chopped
2 strips fresh ginger
3 cups chicken stock *or* water
freshly ground black pepper
3–4 chicken *or* pork sausages
freshly chopped fresh chives for
  garnishing (optional)

*A lovely thick, country-style soup with a similar sweetness to
pumpkin soup and a bright orange colour, it can be eaten the
moment it is made, or kept for several days. A number of
poultry shops stock chicken sausages but if you do not have
access to these a good quality pork sausage will do just as well.
The kind of sweet potato I use for this soup is the very orange
one, often called kumara.*

- Put the sweet potato and potato into a saucepan with the
  ginger and stock, and bring to the boil. Leave to cook gently
  until the potato and sweet potato are quite tender.

- In a blender or food processor, blend the contents of the
  saucepan to a purée. If too thick you can add a dash more
  stock or water. Return the purée to the saucepan, season
  with pepper, and gently reheat.

- While the soup is cooking, put the sausages into a saucepan
  and cover with cold water. Bring them slowly to the boil,
  and simmer (just a few bubbles should occasionally form on
  the edge) until they are cooked. Chicken sausages will take
  about 10 minutes; thick pork sausages may take a few
  minutes longer.

- Drain the sausages. Any fat will have come away in the
  water.

- As soon as you can handle the sausages, cut a slash down the
  length of each one and peel away the skin, which may be
  tough. Cut the sausages into thick slices and add to the soup.

- Serve the soup plain or scatter a dusting of chopped chives
  on the top.

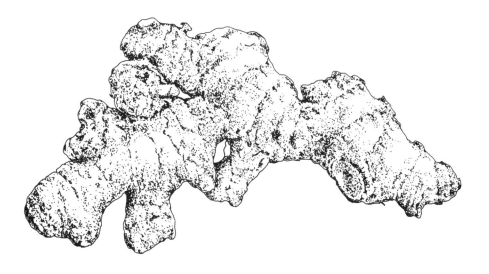

Mushroom Soup with Pine Nuts

Serves 4

30 g butter
1 tablespoon olive oil
⅓ cup chopped frozen onion
1 clove garlic, roughly chopped
250 g mushrooms
3 cups chicken stock
1 tablespoon tomato paste
1 tablespoon dry sherry *or* medium-
  dry sherry
45 g pine nuts
extra tablespoon olive oil

The earthiness of mushrooms and the richness of pine nuts combine well in this soup. Leave time to chop the pine nuts, however; whole nuts will sink to the bottom of the soup bowl, while chopped ones will stay on top.

- Melt the butter with the oil in a saucepan. Add the onion and garlic and let them soften while dicing, chopping or slicing the mushrooms.
- Add the mushroom to the saucepan, turn up the heat and cook for a couple of minutes.
- Tip in the stock, stir in the tomato paste and simmer gently for 5 minutes.
- Transfer the mushroom mixture to a blender or food processor. Purée, return to the saucepan and stir in the sherry. Keep warm.
- In a frying pan, cook the pine nuts in the extra oil, stirring constantly, until golden brown. Drain, then chop the pine nuts into chunky pieces.
- Pour the soup into warmed bowls and top with pine nuts.

Spinach Soup with Blue Cheese

Serves 4

2 teaspoons olive oil
¼ cup pine nuts
1 × 250-g packet frozen spinach
¼ cup chopped frozen onion
1 clove garlic, roughly chopped
1 tablespoon olive oil
3 cups chicken stock
½ cup cream
salt
freshly ground black pepper
60 g Stilton *or* a rich, creamy blue
  cheese

The base of this soup is quick and simple. The addition of creamy, pungent Stilton lifts it out of the ordinary. Don't be tempted to heat the soup once the cheese has been added: heating spoils the texture of the Stilton and may cause it to curdle.

- Heat the 2 teaspoons olive oil in a frying pan and cook the pine nuts, stirring them constantly, until they are golden. Drain on kitchen paper and chop roughly when cool.
- In a saucepan, cook the spinach, onion, garlic and 1 tablespoon olive oil until the spinach has softened.
- Add the stock to the saucepan and bring to the boil. Reduce the heat and cook gently for about 5 minutes.
- Process or blend the soup and return to the saucepan.
- Add the cream, and heat through. Check seasoning.
- Break the cheese into tiny pieces. Pour the soup into bowls and dot the top with the cheese, which will melt by the time the soup is eaten.
- Scatter pine nuts over the soup and serve.

Avocado, Bacon and Caviar

Serves 4

200 g bacon, rind removed
1 large *or* 2 small avocados (about
  250 g)
1 tablespoon lemon juice
a few drops Tabasco
2 tablespoons mayonnaise
pepper
4 lettuce leaves
60 g red caviar

This first course was a creation born of necessity. One evening I suddenly had four guests and one avocado, which although huge could not be easily served in any way except diced, which didn't seem very exciting. With crispy bacon strips and a coating of pink caviar it made a very pretty entrance and the saltiness of both became a good foil for the rich, velvety smoothness of avocado.

- Cut the bacon into fine strips and cook gently in a dry frying pan until crisp. Drain on kitchen paper.

- Cut the avocado into halves, twist and it will come away from the stone. Peel the avocado and cut into dice.

- Mix the lemon juice with the Tabasco and mayonnaise, and season with pepper. Do not use salt, as the bacon and caviar provide plenty.

- Shred the lettuce very finely and place as a base in small bowls or dishes.

- Divide the avocado over the top of the lettuce.

- Scatter the bacon over the avocado and put the pink caviar on top.

NOTE You can prepare the avocado and refrigerate, covered, for 1 hour, but only finish the dish with the bacon and caviar when ready to serve.

Avocado and Curried Mushroom Custard

Serves 4

185 g mushrooms
45 g butter
2 teaspoons curry powder
salt
1 avocado
3 tablespoons finely chopped spring
  onion
3 large eggs
½ cup cream
extra salt
pepper
1 tablespoon tomato sauce

This dish has the same appearance as a quiche without the pastry crust, so it is much faster to make. Bake it in a china quiche dish if you intend to serve it at the table. Never reheat it, as avocado becomes bitter if cooked for too long.

- Grease a 20-cm quiche dish.

- Cut the stalks of the mushrooms level with the caps and slice the mushrooms thickly.

- Melt the butter in a frying pan and cook the mushroom over a high heat until softened. This should only take 1 minute. Add the curry powder and continue to cook for another minute. Season with salt.

- Spread the mushroom over the base of the prepared quiche dish.

- Cut the avocado into halves, twist and it will come away from the stone. Peel the avocado and cut into slices. Arrange over the mushroom and then scatter the spring onion on top.

- Beat the eggs with the cream. Add salt, pepper and tomato sauce and pour over the avocado.

- Preheat the oven to 180°C. Bake the quiche for about 25 minutes or until it has lightly set. Leave to rest for 5 minutes before cutting into slices.

Bean Patties with Coriander

Serves 4

1 × 450-g can cannellini beans
1 cup breadcrumbs made from stale bread
1 egg
½ cup grated carrot
3 spring onion tops, finely chopped
¼ cup freshly chopped coriander sprigs
½ teaspoon chilli sauce *or* a good dash of Tabasco
2 tablespoons light olive oil

This is a nourishing dish with an interesting mealy texture. If you cannot find cannellini beans, other canned beans, such as kidney beans, can be used for this dish. Be sure to rinse the beans very well before use, otherwise the patty mixture will be too wet. This recipe makes about 12 small patties.

Serve these patties on their own or with a fresh tomato sauce to which a few sprigs of coriander have been added at the finish. They are also excellent served with Tiny Tomatoes with Basil, Olives and Capers (see page 145).

- Drain the cannellini beans, rinse well and leave them to stand in a strainer for a couple of minutes.

- Put the breadcrumbs into a bowl, break the egg into them and mix with the grated carrot.

- Put the beans into a food processor and process. I like to leave just a few chunky pieces for texture but have the rest puréed.

- Transfer the bean purée to the bowl with the breadcrumb mixture and add the spring onion, coriander and chilli sauce. Mix well. Chill for about 20 minutes to firm.

- Heat the oil in a frying pan and add spoonfuls of the mixture. Flatten each patty down with the back of a damp spoon, and cook gently until golden brown. Turn to cook the other side. Drain on kitchen paper and keep warm while cooking the remaining patties. Serve immediately.

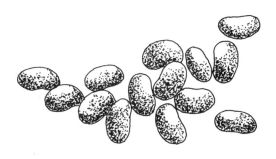

Eggs Baked in Tomato Cases

Serves 4

4 large well-shaped ripe tomatoes
salt
pepper
pinch of sugar
1 tablespoon freshly chopped basil
4 small eggs
extra salt
extra pepper
1 tablespoon cream
4 thin slices St Claire *or* Jarlsberg
  cheese

If you have some end-of-season tomatoes in the garden, this is a lovely way to serve them. Each tomato holds an egg and is topped with nutty cheese. It is best to balance each tomato in a small individual dish when cooking these, because if a ripe tomato splits the egg leaks out. A good breakfast or light lunch dish, it can be eaten just with plain hot toast or served with slices of ham or crisp bacon.

- Put the tomatoes on a board and if they do not balance cut a very small section from the base. Remove a thick slice from the top and scoop out all of the seeds and a little flesh.

- Season the tomatoes with salt, pepper and sugar and put a little basil inside each one.

- Place the tomatoes in small individual ovenproof dishes.

- Break the eggs, one at a time, into a saucer and gently pour into the tomatoes. Season.

- Put 1 teaspoon of cream on the top of each tomato and then 1 slice of cheese over that to completely cover the top.

- Preheat the oven to 180°C. Bake the tomatoes for about 15 to 20 minutes or until the egg has just set and the tomatoes are soft. Be careful not to cook until the egg becomes firm. When the egg is ready the top begins to puff under the cheese.

- Remove the tomatoes from the oven and leave to rest for 30 seconds before serving.

Eggs in Vinaigrette Sauce with Caviar

Serves 4

6 large hard-boiled eggs
4 tablespoons light olive oil
1 tablespoon white wine vinegar
2 tablespoons finely chopped white
  onion
1 teaspoon French mustard
salt
pepper
1 tablespoon sour cream
45 g black caviar
45 g red caviar
several sprigs parsley

This is a tasty first course that can look quite spectacular if you use both black and red caviar and carefully stripe them over the dish.

- Cut the eggs into slices and arrange on a flat platter.

- Whisk the oil. vinegar, onion and mustard in a basin. Season, add the sour cream and mix through.

- Spoon the mixture over the top of the sliced egg.

- Arrange the black caviar in a thin stripe, then some red, more black and more red, across the egg. Do this as carefully as you can so they really are stripes and not just scattered. Top with the parsley.

NOTE The sauce can be made in advance and even put on the egg an hour beforehand, but once you decorate with caviar serve quickly as the colours will come away and affect the clean, sharp look of the dish.

Baked Corn Puff

Serves 4

6 rashers bacon, rind removed
2 ripe tomatoes
salt
pepper
3 tablespoons cream

CORN MIXTURE
45 g butter
1½ tablespoons plain flour
1 × 450-g can creamed corn
4 large egg yolks
6 large egg whites
⅓ cup grated Parmesan cheese

As light as a soufflé, this dish makes a lovely first course for six or a light lunch dish for four and is always popular, even for people who are not normally corn devotees. Unfortunately, it does not keep once made – the 'puff' subsides quickly – so this is a last-minute dish.

- Cut the bacon into strips and fry in a frying pan.

- Cut up the tomatoes roughly and add to the pan. Cook for a few minutes, stirring a couple of times. Season well and add the cream. Bring the mixture to the boil and pour into the base of a shallow 5-cup ovenproof dish.

- To prepare the Corn Mixture, melt the butter in a heavy-based saucepan, as the mixture can stick.

- Add the flour to the saucepan and fry until a pale golden colour.

- Add the corn to the saucepan and stir constantly until the corn has come to the boil and thickened. Remove from the heat and cool slightly.

- Add the egg yolks to the saucepan and mix through.

- Beat the egg whites until stiff and fold through the mixture, a third at at time.

- Pour the mixture over the top of the bacon and tomatoes in the ovenproof dish.

- Scatter the top with the cheese.

- Preheat the oven to 180°C. Bake the puff for about 15 to 20 minutes or until very puffed and golden brown on top.

NOTE Do not over-cook the puff to the point where it is firm and dry; it is best when still a little creamy in the centre.

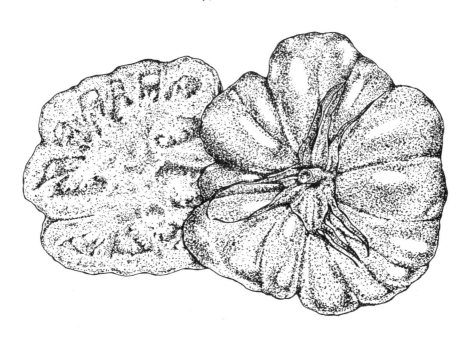

Eggplant and Tomato Antipasto

Serves 4

2 eggplant, thinly sliced
light olive oil
salt
freshly ground black pepper
4 ripe tomatoes, thinly sliced
½ cup virgin *or* light olive oil
1½ tablespoons white wine
    vinegar
1 tablespoon rinsed and chopped
    capers
2 tablespoons freshly chopped
    chives
6 fresh basil leaves, shredded
extra fresh basil leaves for
    garnishing

Autumn is a wonderful time for the ripest, most flavoursome tomatoes and sweet eggplant. Really fresh eggplant feels firm and its skin is taut and glossy. Its flesh is not bitter and does not need to be salted. You can cook the eggplant for this dish a couple of days in advance, if you wish. Prepared at the last moment, the eggplant cools down in about 15 minutes and is ready to serve. As the slices of tomato are placed on top of the eggplant slices, which are all different sizes, it is sensible to buy 2 large and 2 small tomatoes.

This antipasto looks particularly rustic and is nicest presented on a bright flat platter so the slices can be picked up easily.

- If necessary salt the eggplant slices and let them stand for 20 minutes. Rinse and drain well.

- Heat a little oil in a frying pan (use two pans if you are in a hurry) and add the eggplant in one layer. Cook over a fairly high heat until golden. Turn and cook the other side. Transfer to some kitchen paper to drain and season with salt and pepper. Repeat the process until all the eggplant slices have been cooked. Let the eggplant stand for at least 15 minutes before making up the rest of the dish.

- Put the cooled eggplant slices on a platter with the larger ones on the outside and the smaller ones in the centre. Top each with a tomato slice.

- Mix all the remaining ingredients, except the extra basil leaves, and stir with a fork. Spoon a little of this dressing on top of the tomato. The dressing will trickle down the sides while the herbs will remain on top.

- Tuck a few leaves of basil here and there on the platter and serve within an hour.

NOTE Don't chill this dish — it must be served at room temperature.

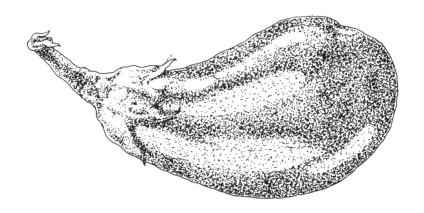

Mushroom Pâté

Serves 4

1 onion, finely diced
2 tablespoons virgin olive oil
250 g mushrooms
2 cloves garlic, roughly chopped
1 tomato, roughly chopped
1 tablespoon tomato paste
1 teaspoon salt
freshly ground black pepper
1 tablespoon freshly chopped
 parsley
1 tablespoon freshly chopped chives

This easy-to-make pâté has all the flavours of autumn and is delicious teamed with crusty bread, toast or crackers. Kept covered, it can be stored in the refrigerator for up to 4 days.

- Put the onion and oil into a frying pan and cook gently while slicing the mushrooms.

- When the onion has softened, add the sliced mushrooms and garlic and cook over a high heat until the mushroom has wilted.

- Add the tomato, tomato paste, salt and pepper. Leave to cook gently for about 5 minutes. If there is a lot of liquid, cook further until it has boiled away.

- Put the mixture into a food processor and process to a thick paste. Taste, and season very well. If the mixture is too dry add a spoonful more olive oil and process once more.

- Remove to a bowl, mix in the parsley and chives and chill for about 20 minutes before serving.

Mushroom Salad with Walnut Dressing

Serves 4

385 g mushrooms
4 tablespoons light olive oil
2 tablespoons walnut oil
2 tablespoons white wine vinegar
2 teaspoons French mustard
2 teaspoons horseradish relish
salt
pepper
2 extra tablespoons light olive oil
½ cup coarsely broken pieces of
 walnut

The flavours of both mushrooms and walnuts gain fullness by the addition of walnut oil. A wonderful rich oil, it needs to be used sparingly because of these very qualities. Use the best walnuts you can buy. If you are not sure of the freshness of packaged walnuts buy fresh ones; it only takes a few minutes to shell them and the difference to the salad is noticeable. This salad serves four as a first course.

- Wipe the tops of the mushrooms, cut the stalks level with the caps and cut into thin slices.

- Mix the oils with the vinegar. Add the mustard, horseradish relish and salt and pepper.

- Mix the oil mixture through the mushroom and leave to marinate for about 15 minutes.

- Heat the extra oil. Add the walnut pieces and fry, stirring constantly, until they are crispy and slightly brown. Be careful not to let them burn as they catch easily. Drain on kitchen paper.

- Serve a small mound of mushroom salad on individual entrée-size plates and scatter with pieces of walnut.

NOTE As the mushroom marinates it will soften. If a lot of liquid accumulates around it, drain some away before using the mushroom in the salad.

Stuffed Mushrooms with Cheese Topping   *Serves 4*

8 large flat mushrooms (about 60 g
  each)
salt
pepper
30 g butter
1 tablespoon light olive oil

STUFFING
4 large mushrooms
reserved stalks from the 8
  mushrooms to be stuffed
30 g butter
1 tablespoon finely chopped shallot
  or onion
1 clove garlic, finely chopped
salt
pepper
2 tablespoons port *or* medium-dry
  sherry
3 tablespoons breadcrumbs made
  from stale bread
60 g St Claire cheese, finely sliced

Buy big mushrooms for stuffing. They should not be too flat, though, or the stuffing will fall over the edges. The ideas for stuffing mushrooms are many: cooked spinach; herbs added to breadcrumbs with butter; chopped walnuts or browned almonds and pine nuts.

- Remove the stalks from the 8 large flat mushrooms and reserve. Season the mushroom caps.

- Melt the butter and heat the oil and brush on the outside of the mushroom caps; this prevents them from wrinkling and drying when cooking.

- Place the mushrooms, cap side down, in a shallow ovenproof dish.

- To make the Stuffing, cut the 4 large mushrooms and their stalks, and the reserved stalks, into small dice.

- Melt the butter and add the mushroom, shallot and garlic. Sauté for a few minutes, stirring occasionally, until the mushroom has softened.

- Season and add the port. Boil until the pan is almost dry.

- Put the mixture into a basin, add the breadcrumbs and press with your fingers to check that it holds together. If not, add a little more butter; if too moist, add more breadcrumbs.

- Fill the mushroom caps with the stuffing and put the cheese slices on top of each one.

- Preheat the oven to 180°C. Bake the mushroms for about 10 minutes or until they are tender and the cheese has melted. Do not over-cook or the mushrooms will collapse.

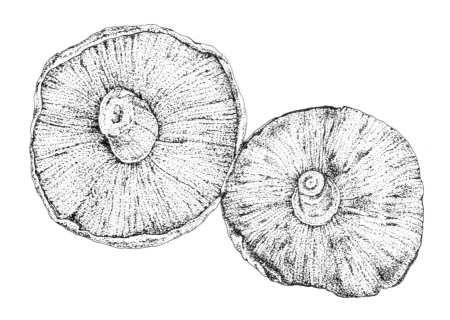

Black Olive Spread

Serves 4

300 g black olives, pitted
2 cloves garlic
125 g pine nuts
1 teaspoon freshly ground black
 pepper
⅓ cup virgin olive oil

Intensely flavoured, this robust spread can be used with some bread as a first course at the dinner table or as a nibble with drinks. Its pungent taste makes it handy for a number of other uses, too. For example, you can dab a little on top of a fresh tomato sauce over pasta, put a teaspoonful in the base of a bowl before ladling in chunky vegetable soup, or spread a thin layer of it on a plain grilled steak.

Be sure to buy olives in brine, not oil, and get stoned olives, otherwise you will spend most of the day removing the pieces of flesh from the stone. This spread keeps well, covered and refrigerated, for about a week.

- Drain the olives and rinse them. Leave for a moment to drain again.

- Crush the garlic and put the olives and garlic into a food processor. Process roughly.

- Add the pine nuts and process again, seasoning with the black pepper. Scrape down the sides – the mixture will be quite thick.

- With the motor running, add enough oil to give a thick consistency suitable for spreading on bread or croutons.

- Check the seasoning. You can add a little more pepper but salt is not usually needed as the olives provide plenty of their own.

- Remove to a storage jar or crock. The spread can be eaten immediately or covered and chilled slightly.

Salmon Slices with a Cucumber Sauce

Serves 4

375-g filleted tail end of salmon
black peppercorns
salt
2 tablespoons lemon juice
1 tablespoon virgin olive oil
1 continental cucumber
1 teaspoon sugar
1 tablespoon vinegar
¼ cup sour cream
¼ cup mayonnaise
2 tablespoons finely chopped fresh
  chervil, chives *or* dill

Although this is served as a cool dish, the salmon should be cooked at the last moment. The fish is plated while warm and the refreshing cucumber sauce is spooned on top before serving. The salmon remains very moist and succulent and as it is rich one slice, or two if tiny, is ample for a first course. A fillet in one piece from the tail end is ideal for this dish.

- With a sharp knife cut the salmon on the diagonal into slices about 1.5 cm thick. Slide the slices off the skin and put them onto a dinner plate.

- Crush some black peppercorns very coarsely and press onto both sides of each salmon slice. Season the salmon lightly with salt on one side.

- Mix the lemon juice with the oil and brush a little on one side only of each salmon slice.

- Peel the cucumber, cut into halves lengthwise and remove the seeds. Grate the cucumber into a bowl and add the sugar and vinegar. Stand for 5 minutes, then drain or squeeze out any liquid.

- Preheat the griller with a flat baking tray underneath it.

- Combine the sour cream and mayonnaise, then add the grated cucumber and the chopped herbs, and mix. Do this only 5 minutes before serving or the sauce will become very wet.

- Quickly brush the hot baking tray with oil and grill the salmon slices on the side brushed with the lemon juice and oil mixture. There is no need to turn the fish. Be very careful not to overcook it – the cooking process takes 2 to 3 minutes at the most. Transfer the salmon slices to plates, spoon the cucumber sauce over the fish, and serve.

Salmon Stew

Serves 4

375 g Alantic salmon *or* ocean trout
4 cups water
salt
pepper
2 tablespoons light olive oil
1 large onion, finely chopped
2 large potatoes, cut into dice
1 small red capsicum, cut into dice
4 large ripe tomatoes, roughly
 chopped
12 basil leaves
dash of lemon juice

This pinky mixture of small chunks of Atlantic salmon in a sea of tomato could be described as soup or stew. A substantial dish, it could double as a one-course meal with some crusty bread. Buy a flat tail-end piece, not a cutlet with bones, for this dish.

- Carefully remove the flesh from the skin by sliding the knife between them (or ask the fishmonger to do this for you).

- Place the skin in a saucepan, add the water, season, and bring slowly to the boil.

- Heat the oil in a saucepan, add the onion and cook for 1 minute.

- Add the potato and capsicum to the pan and fry for 1 minute. Put the lid on the pan and leave to cook for about 10 minutes or until the vegetables have softened.

- Cut the salmon into dice, discarding any bones.

- Put the tomato into the potato mixture, turn up the heat and cook quickly for a few minutes or until a thick sauce forms.

- Strain the liquid from the salmon skin into the sauce, bring to the boil, add the salmon and cook for about 1 minute.

- Put the lid on the pan, remove the pan from the heat and leave to rest for 1 minute. Add the basil and gently stir, and add the lemon juice to freshen the flavours.

Sautéd Tomatoes with Spiced Dressing

Serves 4

4 tomatoes
1 tablespoon virgin olive oil
salt
pepper
a little sugar

DRESSING
6 tablespoons light olive oil
2 tablespoons white wine vinegar
1 tablespoon finely chopped capers
1 tablespoon finely chopped sweet-
 sour cucumber
1 clove garlic, crushed

Tomatoes cooked in oil have a lovely texture and flavour when used in a salad, and they absorb the dressing. While it is best to use ripe tomatoes that are full of true tomato flavour, this method gives the not so ripe and tasty ones a bit more zest.

- Trim both ends from the tomatoes. Cut the tomatoes into halves horizontally.

- Heat the oil in a frying pan and when very hot add the tomatoes.

- Cook the tomatoes, turning once, until softened on the outside and showing specks of brown.

- Place the tomatoes on a serving plate and season with salt, pepper and a pinch of sugar.

- To make the Dressing, mix the oil and vinegar in a basin. Add the remaining ingredients and spoon over the tomatoes while they are warm.

- Leave the tomatoes to cool; do not refrigerate or the flavour is dulled.

Salad of Witlof with Cress and Orange

Serves 4

2 witlof
ice cubes
½ bunch watercress
2 medium-sized oranges

DRESSING
1 tablespoon French mustard
2 teaspoons sugar
3 tablespoons light olive oil
1 tablespoon white wine vinegar
2 tablespoons orange juice

Known as 'witloof' by the Belgians who developed it, occasionally called 'chicory' and frequently 'endive', this vegetable is usually known as 'witlof' in Australia and is now grown almost all year round. It is a crisp, slightly bitter vegetable that is equally good cooked or raw in salads. The paler the tips the better the witlof; the darker the green colour the more bitter the taste. (See colour plate opposite.)

- Cut the base from the witlof and cut away the top leafy part. Cut each stalk into several long strips and place in water containing a few ice cubes to crisp.

- Wash the watercress well, remove the tips and discard stalks or any tough sections. Pat dry on kitchen paper.

- Peel the oranges, removing all the bitter white pith. Separate the segments, place in a basin, and chill.

- Mix all the Dressing ingredients together, whisking with a fork.

- To assemble the salad, put the witlof strips around the edge of a platter, or individual plates, and heap the watercress in the centre. Spoon the Dressing over both and arrange the orange segments on top of the watercress.

OPPOSITE PAGE ▶
Salad of Witlof with Cress and Orange is served with a tangy dressing flavoured with orange and mustard (this page).

MAIN COURSES

Quail with Turnips and Ginger

Serves 4

8 quail
60 g butter
1 clove garlic, crushed
salt
pepper
8 baby turnips
¼ cup water
2 teaspoons grated fresh ginger
extra salt
3 teaspoons sugar
30 g butter

Large turnips are not suitable for this dish, as they are too strong, but baby turnips are sold in speciality greengrocers and at most markets. (See colour plate opposite.)

- Pat the quail dry.

- Melt butter and brush on the quail. Season well and pack into a metal dish such as a cake tin so they fit closely.

- Preheat the oven to 200°C. Cook the quail for about 15 minutes. Remove from the oven and cover with foil. Leave aside for 10 minutes.

- Cut away all but a little of the turnips' greenery. Peel the turnips, cut into quarters (leave whole if tiny) and place in a saucepan. Cover with cold water and bring to the boil. Cook for 1 minute and drain.

- Return the turnip to the saucepan and add the ¼ cup of water, ginger, salt and sugar. Cover, and cook for about 12 minutes or until tender.

- Remove the lid of the saucepan, add the butter, and cook over a high heat until the turnip has a syrupy glaze over it.

- Cut each quail in half. Place, flat side down, on a serving platter and pour the turnip and glaze over the top.

◀ *OPPOSITE PAGE*
Quail with Turnips and Ginger (this page) teams well with Sautéd Lettuce and Onion (page 137) and julienne carrots for an autumn repast.

Fillet Steak with Cucumber and Tomato

Serves 4

4 pieces fillet steak
oil
salt
15-cm-long piece cucumber
250 g ripe tomatoes
30 g butter
2 teaspoons Worcestershire sauce
1 clove garlic, crushed
extra salt
pepper
½ teaspoon sugar

Light in flavour, cucumber is usually associated with salads rather than hot dishes but it has an interesting texture and combines well with tomatoes in a sauce.

- Trim the steaks of any fat or sinew and brush both sides of each one with oil.

- Heat a saucepan containing a little water and season with salt.

- Peel the piece of cucumber and cut into halves lengthwise. Scoop out all the seeds and cut the cucumber into small dice. Cook in the water for 3 to 4 minutes or until slightly softened.

- Put the tomatoes into a basin and drain the cucumber in a sieve over the top. Leave to stand for 10 seconds and then peel the tomatoes. Cut into dice.

- Melt the butter in a saucepan. Add the cucumber and tomato and cook for about 5 minutes or until you have a thick sauce. Add the Worcestershire sauce and garlic. Check seasonings and add sugar. (The sauce can be reheated.)

- Heat a frying pan. When smoking hot, add the steaks and cook, turning, until they are brown and crusty on the outside but still pink inside. Season.

- Put a little sauce on the bottom of each plate and top with a steak.

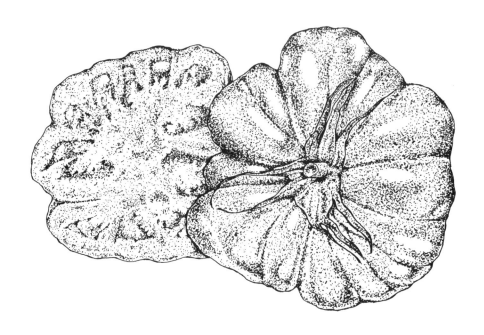

Beef in Diane Sauce

Serves 6

6 pieces fillet steak
1 tablespoon oil
1 shallot
2 cloves garlic
small handful parsley sprigs
1 tablespoon Worcestershire sauce
½ cup chicken stock
45 g butter

For years when I was growing up one of the specialities of sophisticated restaurants was Steak Diane, which was usually cooked with a fanfare by the head waiter at the table and filled the restaurant with the aromas of garlic and Worcestershire sauce: fine if you were the person eating the dish, not so desirable for all the other guests. This kind of ostentatious cooking is rarely seen now.

The dish can be good and is incredibly quick and easy. I lighten the sauce with stock and use a good quality steak.

- Trim any fat or sinew from the beef and flatten it down. If very thick, it is best to cut the beef through the centre and make two flatter portions.

- Heat the oil in a large frying pan or two medium-sized pans.

- Add the beef to the pan. While it is cooking on the first side, chop the shallot and crush the garlic. Chop the parsley finely.

- Keep turning the meat. Altogether it takes about 4 to 5 minutes depending on the thickness.

- Remove the meat to a warm plate and put another plate on top to retain the heat.

- Add the shallot and garlic to the pan. Fry for 30 seconds and then add the Worcestershire sauce and stir (it will sizzle madly). Add the stock and stir to get up any brown specks.

- Remove the pan from the heat, add the parsley and butter, and leave the butter to melt.

- Some juices may have run out of the meat. Pour these into the sauce and then put the meat back, turning each piece over so it is coated on both sides with sauce. Serve immediately and spoon just a dribble of sauce on top.

Veal Scaloppini Mediterranean

Serves 4

SAUCE
boiling water
250 g tomatoes
45 g butter
1 teaspoon sugar
pepper
1 tablespoon freshly choppped basil
1 tablespoon freshly chopped parsley
several anchovy fillets, roughly chopped
1 tablespoon capers

VEAL
4 veal scaloppini
seasoned plain flour
3 tablespoons light olive oil

One of the quickest of all veal dishes to cook, scaloppini will toughen if cooked slowly and dry if over-cooked, so watch it all the time. It is best to have the sauce ready rather than keep the meat waiting.

- Pour boiling water over the tomatoes and leave to stand for 10 seconds. Peel them and cut into small dice.

- Melt the butter in a saucepan. Add the tomato, sugar and pepper and cook over a high heat for a couple of minutes.

- Add the basil, parsley, chopped anchovy and capers to the pan. Cook until the tomato has softened but keep the sauce light and fresh. You can reheat it as needed.

- If the scaloppini are not very thin, place between plastic wrap and pound until they are an even thickness. Most butchers will have done this for you.

- Dust the scaloppini with the seasoned flour and transfer to a plate.

- Heat the oil in a large frying pan. When very hot add the veal, taking care not to crowd the pan. Do two at a time if you need to. Keep the scaloppini warm in the oven while you do the remainder. When cooked on one side turn over. They should only take a couple of minutes.

- To serve, drain the veal on kitchen paper and then put onto plates with a little Sauce in the centre of each scaloppini.

Pork Chops with Apple and Cider

Serves 4

4 large *or* 8 small pork chops
a little oil
salt
pepper
1 large cooking apple
30 g butter
1 cup apple cider
pinch of ground cinnamon
3 tablespoons sultanas
2 strips lemon rind
1 teaspoon cornflour *or* arrowroot
2 tablespoons water

The combination of new season's apple and cider cuts the richness of the pork. The new pork cuts contain much less fat but for this reason pork chops can dry if you cook them for too long, so check them carefully.

- Trim the rind from the chops.

- Brush the base of a frying pan with the oil. Heat, add the chops, and brown on both sides. Drain on kitchen paper. Season well.

- Peel and core the apple and cut into thin slices.

- Wipe out the pan. Melt the butter, add the apple slices and cook, stirring, for 1 minute.

- Pour the apple cider into the pan. Add the cinnamon, sultanas and lemon rind, and bring to the boil.

- Arrange the chops in a shallow casserole dish. They can overlap a little. Pour the apple and sauce over the top.

- Preheat the oven to 180°C. Cover the dish and bake for about 30 minutes or until the meat is tender. Baste the chops once or turn them over during cooking.

- Mix the cornflour with the water and add some spoonfuls of juices from the meat. Mix into the meat. The sauce should thicken in the warmth of the oven, but give it a shake so it is even.

- Serve the pork with the apple slices and sultanas spooned on top. You can remove the lemon rind or leave it in.

Pork Chops with Mustard and Chive Sauce   *Serves 4*

4 large *or* 8 small pork chops
2 tablespoons seasoned plain flour
1 tablespoon light olive oil

SAUCE
¾ cup cream
1 tablespoon chopped shallot
1 tablespoon French mustard
3 tablespoons freshly chopped chives
2 tablespoons dry white wine
salt
pepper

When you have a combination of cream and pork in a dish the flavour is delicious but rich. Such food is often best reserved as a lunch dish, or prepared as a main course in the evening only if the rest of the meal is fresh and light. Occasionally I poach some prunes in a little strained tea and place one on top of each chop before serving.

- Trim the rind and fat from the chops.

- Dust the chops with the seasoned flour.

- Heat the oil in a frying pan, add the chops, and cook until they have changed colour on both sides. Turn down the heat and continue cooking for another 15 minutes or until tender, turning several times.

- To make the Sauce, put the cream, shallot, mustard, 2 tablespoons of the chives, wine, salt and pepper into a small saucepan, and cook for a few minutes or until it lightly coats the back of a spoon.

- Set aside and cover to keep warm.

- To serve, drain the chops well and place on heated plates. Spoon the sauce on the chops and scatter the remaining chives on top.

Ham Steaks with Mushroom Sauce

Serves 6

6 ham steaks *or* thick slices ham
30 g butter
125 g mushrooms, cut into thick
  slices
¾ cup dry white wine
½ cup port
boiling water
1 large ripe tomato
1 clove garlic, crushed
pepper
2 teaspoons cornflour
3 tablespoons grated Parmesan
  cheese

There are many more interesting ways to serve ham than simply with the traditional accompaniments of pineapple or mustard sauce. For instance, mushrooms, garlic, tomato and cheese blend into a very flavoursome sauce. The dish can be prepared in advance and later baked in the oven so it makes an easy main course for a dinner or party. You could use portions of leftover ham or buy thick portions from your butcher.

- Place the ham steaks, slightly overlapping, in a shallow ovenproof dish.

- Melt the butter in a frying pan and add the mushroom. Cook for a couple of minutes or until wilted. Add the wine and port, and cook until reduced by half.

- Pour boiling water over the tomato, leave for 10 seconds and then peel. Cut into small dice, and mix into the sauce with the garlic and pepper.

- Mix the cornflour with sufficient water to make a thin paste.

- Bring the sauce to the boil, add the cornflour paste and cook until thickened. Pour the sauce over the ham and scatter the cheese on top.

- Preheat the oven to 180°C. Cook the steaks for about 15 minutes or until the ham is heated and the sauce reduced.

NOTE Do not leave this dish in the oven once the ham is heated or the salt will intensify.

Chicken Breasts with Cherries

Serves 4

4 chicken breasts, boned and
  skinned
seasoned plain flour
45 g butter
1 × 450-g can cherries
⅓ cup dry red wine
½ cup orange juice
several strips lemon rind
1 tablespoon port

Cherries were once a very fashionable accompaniment to duck. They are not often served with chicken but you will find they are very good, and they make a colourful as well as an interesting change.

- Dip the chicken breasts in the seasoned flour.

- Melt the butter in a frying pan. Add the chicken and cook gently, turning until the outside has changed colour. The chicken will still be raw in the centre. Place in a shallow ovenproof dish.

- Drain the cherries and reserve the juice. Put ⅓ cup of reserved juice from the cherries into a basin, add the red wine, orange juice and rind, and pour into the frying pan in which the chicken was cooked. Bring to the boil and pour over the chicken breasts.

- Preheat the oven to 180°C. Bake the chicken for about 12 to 15 minutes or until it is cooked.

- Stone 16 cherries and put the stoned cherries on top of the chicken for the last minute of cooking so they heat through.

Chicken Breasts with Camembert

Serves 4

4 chicken breasts, boned and
  skinned
salt
pepper
125 g Camembert cheese
plain flour
1 egg
extra salt
breadcrumbs made from stale bread
45 g butter
2 tablespoons light olive oil

The Camembert stuffing melts into a creamy layer in the centre of the chicken. Use the cheese directly from the refrigerator so it is firm and easier to use.

- With a wooden rolling pin, flatten each chicken breast between plastic wrap so it is an even thickness.

- Season with salt and pepper.

- Cut the cheese into thick slices.

- Put some flour onto a piece of greaseproof paper. Beat the egg with a pinch of salt. Place the breadcrumbs on another sheet of greaseproof paper.

- Put some cheese on one side of each chicken breast, fold over the other side to enclose, and skewer with fine poultry skewers or toothpicks.

- Dip the chicken into the flour, egg and breadcrumbs. Pat the breadcrumbs on well, and refrigerate the chicken for 10 minutes.

- Heat the oil in the frying pan and when very hot add the chicken and cook over a medium heat for about 15 minutes. If the outside is browning too much before the inside cooks, turn the heat to low.

- Serve with Apple Sauce (see page 110).

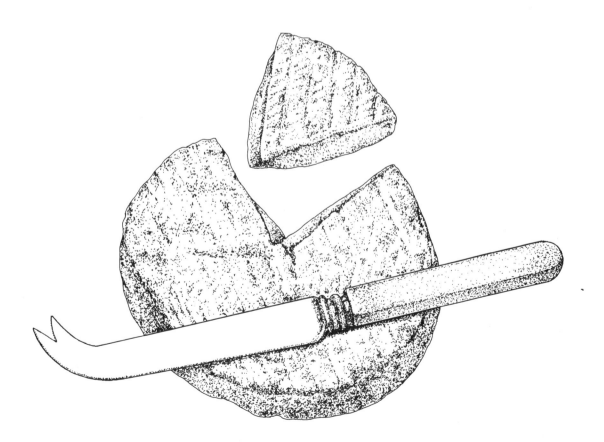

Chicken in Garlic Sauce

Serves 4

30 g butter
1 tablespoon light olive oil
4 large *or* 8 small chicken portions
  (such as drumsticks, thighs, wings,
  pieces of breast on the bone)
salt
pepper
15 cloves garlic, unpeeled
1 bay leaf
2 teaspoons freshly chopped
  rosemary
½ cup dry white wine

Since the time of Hippocrates garlic has topped the list of cures for ailments as disparate as the common cold and leprosy. A bulb worn around the neck would protect the wearer against witches; Romans and Elizabethans ate garlic in the belief that it was a potent aphrodisiac.

The way garlic is handled determines the final taste of the dish. Crushed raw, it may have an explosive pungency, while the same quantity poached or boiled will give a gentle almost buttery flavour. In this dish there is a lot of garlic but it is digestible and sweet, so do not be deterred.

- Heat the butter and oil in a frying pan.

- Sauté the chicken portions until they are a brown colour on the outside. As they cook, transfer them to an ovenproof casserole dish that has a tight-fitting lid. Season well with salt and pepper.

- Drain away any oil from the frying pan. Add the garlic, cook for 1 minute, shaking the pan several times so the cloves move around. Add the bay leaf, rosemary and wine.

- Pour the liquid and the garlic from the pan over the chicken.

- Preheat the oven to 180°C. Cover the casserole dish with the lid and bake for about 35 minutes for drumsticks, thighs and wings; about 20 minutes for chicken breasts.

- When cooked, remove the chicken portions to a warm plate and put another one on top to keep in the heat.

- Pour the liquid and garlic from the dish through a sieve and press down to get out all the juices from the garlic. If the sauce is too thin you can boil it for a few minutes to reduce.

- Serve the chicken with the garlic sauce on top.

Chicken Baked in Port and Mushroom Sauce   *Serves 4*

1.5 kg even-sized chicken portions
  (such as drumsticks, thighs, wings,
  pieces of breast on the bone)
30 g butter
1 tablespoon light olive oil
1 onion, finely chopped
125 g small mushrooms
1 cup port
salt
pepper
½ cup thick cream

Quite a rich dish, the port and cream combination fills the kitchen with enticing aromas and wonderfully transforms the flesh of the chicken during baking.

- Check the chicken portions are the same size. If uneven, cut to make them the same so they will cook evenly.

- Melt the butter and heat the oil in a frying pan and add the chicken portions, a few at a time. As they change colour all over transfer to an ovenproof casserole dish.

- Scatter the onion over the chicken.

- Add the mushrooms to the same pan in which the chicken was cooked, and toss until coated with butter and oil. Put over the chicken.

- Discard any fat or oil in the frying pan, add the port and bring to the boil. Pour into the casserole dish, season if necessary and cover the dish.

- Preheat the oven to 180°C. Bake the chicken for about 30 minutes or until the chicken is tender. Remove the chicken to a warm dish and cover.

- Pour the sauce, along with the onion and mushroom, into a large saucepan. Add the cream, and boil for a few minutes to thicken the sauce a little.

- Put the chicken in the saucepan with the sauce and keep warm until ready to serve.

Chicken Wings in Green Peppercorn Sauce   *Serves 4*

1 kg chicken wings
¼ cup lemon juice
2 tablespoons water
1 tablespoon dark soy sauce
1 teaspoon grated fresh ginger
1 clove garlic, crushed
1 tablespoon brown sugar
2 teaspoons green peppercorns,
  drained and lightly crushed
¼ cup chopped spring onion
water (if necessary)

They may be awkward to eat but their sweet flavour and lovely gelatinous texture make chicken wings the best portion of the chicken. The ingredients in this dish combine to good effect: lemon has a great affinity with chicken; the spices colour and glaze the wings; and there is a firm tongue-tingling bite from the addition of green peppercorns.

- Place the chicken wings in a shallow casserole dish with a lid.

- Mix the remaining ingredients, except the spring onion, in a saucepan. Bring to the boil.

- Preheat the oven to 180°C. Pour the mixture over the chicken and put the lid on the dish. Cook about 20 minutes.

- Remove the lid and cook for a further 15 to 20 minutes or until the chicken is quite tender and the sauce glazed. If the pan becomes dry, add a few spoonfuls of water.

- Transfer the chicken wings and sauce to a serving dish, and scatter the spring onion on top.

Split Chicken with Onions

Serves 4

1 × 1.5-kg chicken
salt
pepper
60 g butter
3 onions

Chicken (split for fast cooking) placed on a pile of onion segments gains flavour from the roasting onion while the onion becomes permeated with juices from the chicken.

- Remove the wing tip from the chicken, cut alongside the backbone and spread out, pressing down firmly to flatten the chicken. Remove any fat.

- Season generously on both sides with salt and pepper.

- Melt the butter and brush a little of it over the top of the chicken.

- Peel the onions, cut into halves and then segments like an apple. You should get eight segments from each onion.

- Place the onion in a basin, pour the remaining melted butter over the top and season with salt and pepper. Place the onion in a mound in a shallow metal baking dish.

- Put the chicken, skin side up, on the onion, ensuring all the onion is covered.

- Preheat the oven to 180°C. Bake the chicken for about 45 to 50 minutes, basting several times with the juices.

- Remove the chicken from the oven, cut into four portions and spoon the onion alongside.

NOTE Check the onion as it cooks. If it begins to caramelise and darken too much, add ¼ cup of water to the baking dish to stop it burning.

Fish Fillets with Spring Onion and Ginger   *Serves 4*

½ cup water
1 tablespoon soy sauce
1 tablespoon sugar
1 tablespoon white wine vinegar
1 clove garlic, crushed *or* finely
  chopped
2 teaspoons grated fresh ginger
½ cup chopped spring onion
2 teaspoons cornflour
4 × 125-g fish fillets (such as
  bream *or* snapper)
seasoned plain flour
1 large egg
peanut oil

Any fish fillets suitable for pan frying are suitable for this dish. The flavour is quite dominating so fine, delicate fish such as whiting are wasted. Fish such as bream or snapper are ideal.

- Put the water, soy sauce, sugar, vinegar, garlic and ginger into a small saucepan and bring to the boil.

- Add the spring onion to the pan and cook for a couple of minutes.

- Mix the cornflour with a little water to a thin paste. Pour into the sauce and bring to the boil, stirring until it thickens. Leave the sauce aside and keep warm while cooking the fish, or reheat it as needed.

- Dust the fish fillets with the seasoned flour. Shake away any excess.

- Beat the egg on a flat plate.

- Heat enough oil to cover the base of a shallow frying pan.

- Dip the fish into the egg.

- Add the fish to the hot oil, one fillet at a time so the heat level is retained, and cook until golden on the outside and cooked through. Timing will depend on the thickness of the fish. Thin fillets take 3 to 4 minutes; thick ones about 7 minutes. Drain on kitchen paper.

- Serve the fillets with a good spoonful of sauce on top of each one.

NOTE This method of coating fish gives it a fine light casing.

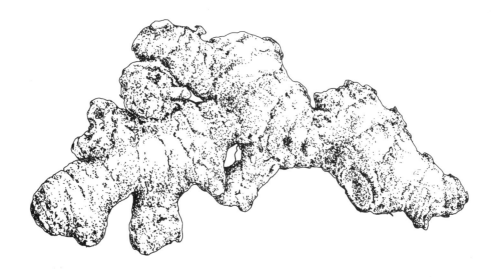

Baked Spiced Fish

Serves 6

6 fish fillets *or* small whole fish
  (cleaned, heads left on)
3 tablespoons sesame seeds
2 tablespoons soy sauce
2 teaspoons sugar
1 teaspoon dark sesame oil
1 large clove garlic, crushed
1 teaspoon grated fresh ginger
dash of Tabasco *or* chilli sauce
1 tablespoon vegetable oil *or* light
  olive oil

*Either fillets of fish or whole small fish can be used in this dish.
The spicy topping has such flavour that you can use fish that
may be a little bland, but the spices will stand up with
authority to a rich fish, too. Small whole fish such as bream,
baby snapper and dory are ideal, and you can use fillets of
snapper, dory, blue eye and trevally. The fish can either be
grilled or baked, and I like it served on a bed of stir-fried bean
shoots.*

- Pat the fish dry.

- Put the sesame seeds in a dry frying pan and cook until
  golden (be careful as the seeds change colour quickly). Give
  them a stir with a fork or shake the pan several times.

- Put the seeds into a mortar and pestle, and grind coarsely; or
  put on a board and grind using the end of a rolling pin. It is
  too small a quantity to put into a blender or food processor
  unless you have a spice attachment that grinds.

- Place the seeds in a basin. Add the remaining ingredients and
  mix.

- Spread the mixture over the top of the fish.

- Place the fish on a lightly greased piece of baking paper on a
  flat baking tray; or put the fish on the rack of your grill.

- Preheat the oven to 180°C. Cook the fish fillets for about 8
  minutes; whole fish for about 12 minutes. The timing
  depends on the thickness of the fish. If grilling the fish, brush
  just a little of the mixture on one side, grill that side for
  about 3 to 4 minutes, turn over and brush with the
  remainder of the mixture. Grill again for about 2 minutes.
  Again, the timing depends on the thickness of the fish.

Fusilli with Smoked Trout and Caviar Sauce   *Serves 4*

250 g fusilli pasta
salt
1 tablespoon lemon juice
250 g smoked trout
2 tablespoons finely chopped
  shallot
45 g butter
1¼ cups cream
¼ cup freshly chopped chervil *or*
  chives
60 g red caviar
plenty of freshly ground black
  pepper

Fusilli are little spirals of pasta, which are ideal for capturing creamy trout and pink caviar in their curled sections. This is a rich dish, so serve a small quantity. Do not add salt prematurely as the fish will provide plenty. It is best to wait and taste.

For speed, choose trout that is ready skinned and boned (usually vacuum-packed and sold through delicatessens).

- Heat a large saucepan of water until boiling, add the fusilli and stir so none stick to the base. Salt and leave to cook for about 13 to 15 minutes or until just tender. Test one by tasting. Drain.

- Add the lemon juice and stir through the pasta.

- Prepare the sauce while the pasta is cooking. Break the trout into small portions.

- In a saucepan, heat the chopped shallot with the butter and after a minute add the cream. Bring to the boil and simmer gently for a couple of minutes.

- Add the chervil or chives to the pan and leave aside.

- Pour the sauce over the fusilli and toss gently to coat.

- Place in a big serving dish, dot with the caviar and grind the black pepper on top.

Pasta with Broccoli and Tomatoes

Serves 4

500 g penne *or* other short pasta
375 g broccoli
3 tablespoons virgin olive oil
3 cloves garlic, finely chopped
1 small onion, finely chopped
1 teaspoon ground turmeric
3 tomatoes, roughly diced
2 tablespoons currants
⅓ cup pine nuts
½ cup grated Parmesan cheese
extra grated Parmesan cheese

This is an inexpensive and bright pasta dish. The currants give an occasional burst of sweetness while the pine nuts add a delicious richness.

- Put a large pan of water on to boil. Salt well and cook the pasta until it is *al dente* while you prepare the sauce. Drain the pasta and return it to the saucepan.

- While the pasta is cooking rinse the broccoli and cut into even-sized pieces. Remove the tough end of the stalks. If the stalks are large, peel them.

- Cook the broccoli in salted boiling water for about 5 minutes. Drain and keep ¾ cup of the cooking liquid.

- Heat the oil in a large frying pan, add the garlic and onion and cook until wilted. Add the turmeric and fry for 30 seconds. Add the tomato and cook, covered, for 5 minutes.

- Break or cut the broccoli into small pieces and add to the tomato mixture with the broccoli liquid, currants and pine nuts. Heat through, stirring well, but don't overcook.

- Add the sauce to the pasta and stir in ½ cup grated Parmesan cheese. Serve with more grated cheese on the table.

Spaghetti with Tomato and Anchovy Sauce

Serves 4

1 tablespoon salt
1 tablespoon oil
375 g spaghetti

SAUCE
90 g butter
1 white onion, finely chopped
500 g ripe tomatoes, peeled
60 g pine nuts
pepper
½ teaspoon sugar
45 g anchovy fillets, chopped
3 tablespoons finely chopped fresh
  parsley
½ cup grated Parmesan cheese

There is a lovely mixture of flavours and textures in this sauce – the saltiness of anchovy, the tart and sweet combination of ripe tomatoes and the crunch of pine nuts.

- Bring a large saucepan of water to the boil, add the salt, oil and spaghetti. Cook until just tender, tasting to test the strands.

- Drain the spaghetti and leave aside.

- To make the Sauce, melt half the butter in a saucepan, add the onion and cook until slightly softened.

- Dice the tomatoes while the onion is cooking.

- Add the pine nuts to the onion and fry until golden.

- Add the tomato to the pan.

- Season the mixture with pepper, add the sugar, and cook until thick. It takes about 8 minutes.

- Add the anchovy and parsley to the pan, and taste for seasoning.

- Add the remaining butter to the sauce, mix into the spaghetti and toss.

- Serve with the Parmesan cheese on the table.

Easy Lamb Curry

Serves 4

⅓ cup plain yoghurt
¾ cup water
1 tablespoon tomato paste
2.5-cm piece fresh ginger
4 cloves garlic, peeled and roughly
  chopped
¼ cup water
3 tablespoons peanut oil
750 g lamb, cubed
extra tablespoon peanut oil
  (optional)
1 cinnamon stick
3 cloves
1 tablespoon curry powder
1 teaspoon salt
a little lemon juice

This simple curry has a lovely flavour and a pinky tomato colour. Choose lamb that is not fatty, such as a piece from the leg or perhaps the shoulder. Like most curries this dish can be reheated and its flavour will improve even more with keeping.

- Mix the yoghurt with ¾ cup water and tomato paste.

- Peel the ginger and cut it into a few pieces. Place in a blender or food processor with the garlic and ¼ cup water and purée.

- Heat the oil in a large saucepan or deep-sided frying pan, add the meat a few cubes at a time and cook over a high heat until coloured. As it is done remove the meat to a plate. Repeat the process until all the meat is cooked.

- Add an extra spoonful of oil to the pan if it is dry. Fry the cinnamon stick, cloves and curry powder in the pan for 30 seconds. Tip the ginger and garlic purée into the pan, then the yoghurt mixture. Add the meat and salt and bring to the boil.

- Cook, covered, over a low heat until the meat is tender, about 25 minutes. Remove the lid and cook rapidly to reduce some of the sauce. Season the curry with a little lemon juice to give it a fresh tart taste, and serve.

Marinated Lamb Strips

Serves 4

8 lamb fillets
1 tablespoon lemon juice
2 teaspoons balsamic vinegar *or*
  wine vinegar
½ cup virgin olive oil
2 cloves garlic, roughly chopped
1 tablespoon freshly chopped
  rosemary
freshly ground black pepper
salt

Although lamb can be stronger in autumn than at other times of the year, lamb marinated and baked in a hot oven is moist and sweet. You will need 24 wooden skewers for this dish. When I have plenty in the garden I cut sticks of rosemary from which I remove all but one tuft of the fragrant leaves. I then thread the meat onto these rosemary skewers, which impart extra flavour, look wonderful and make a good conversation piece.

- Remove any shiny sinew from the fillets with a sharp knife. Cut each fillet of lamb into three lengthwise. Place the lamb strips in one layer in a shallow glass dish.

- Mix all the remaining ingredients, except the salt. Pour the marinade over the lamb strips and leave at room temperature for 20 minutes, or refrigerate for up to 24 hours. Turn the lamb strips occasionally in the marinade.

- Preheat the oven to 200°C and put a metal tray in it to heat.

- Thread a lamb strip loosely onto a skewer and repeat the process until all the strips are used. Place the skewered meat on the very hot oven tray. Bake for 8–10 minutes, depending on whether you prefer lamb slightly pink or more well done.

- Scatter the lamb strips with the tiniest bit of salt. Serve immediately as this dish becomes cold quickly.

Lamb Fillets with Redcurrant and Mint   *Serves 4*

2 oranges
⅓ cup redcurrant jelly
1 tablespoon port
1 tablespoon dry English mustard
2 tablespoon lemon juice
salt
pepper
1 tablespoon freshly chopped mint
500 g lamb fillets
a little light olive oil *or* peanut oil
extra salt
extra pepper

Fillet is one of the sweetest cuts of lamb but remove any sinew from the outside of the meat or it will be chewy. Be sure not to over-cook the fillets, which can either be left whole in the slightly sweet minty sauce, or quickly sliced into about three portions before taking the dish to the table. (See colour plate opposite.)

- Remove the rind from one of the oranges and squeeze the juice from both. Place in a saucepan with all the ingredients except the mint and bring to the boil. Cook gently for a couple of minutes. Add the mint.

- Pat the meat dry.

- Heat sufficient oil to film the base of a frying pan. Add the lamb and cook, turning over several times, until crusty brown on the outside and still pink inside. The fillets should only take about 3 to 5 minutes, depending on their size.

- Season the fillets and remove from the pan. Wipe the pan out.

- Pour the sauce into the pan, return the fillets and turn them over so they are coated. Serve the fillets with a little sauce around them.

OPPOSITE PAGE ▶
Lamb Fillets with Redcurrant and Mint, garnished with fine strips of orange rind, are ideal for entertaining (this page). Partnered with Sautéd Potato Cubes (page 140) and Beans with Sesame Seeds (page 131), this dish makes an elegant main course.

DESSERTS

Hot Grilled Figs on a Raspberry Pond   *Serves 4*

12–16 small green figs
¼ cup cream
brown sugar
1 punnet (250 g) raspberries
2 tablespoons castor sugar

When the leaves are becoming dry on the trees and tinged with colour you can buy figs to team with the second crop of autumn raspberries. This dessert is one of my favourite combinations and worth waiting all year to make: sweet hot creamy figs on a cold tart raspberry sauce. I like to use small green figs but other varieties could be substituted. If the figs are small allow four per person; if large, two or three would be sufficient. A few whole raspberries can be dotted on the sauce for added texture. (See colour plate opposite.)

- Peel the outside skin from the figs. Place them in a very shallow dish, or on a piece of foil in a baking dish.

- Place 1 teaspoon of cream on top of each fig.

- Dot ½ teaspoon of brown sugar on each fig.

- Preheat the grill. Place the figs under the grill and cook until they are very hot and the sugar has melted over the top.

- While the figs are cooking, push the raspberries through a sieve, add the castor sugar and stir to soften the sugar.

- Place the raspberry sauce on a platter. Lift the figs from their dish and arrange them on the sauce.

NOTE If large figs are the only type available, peel and cut a deep cross on top before grilling. The figs will open slightly, like a flower, as they heat.

◀   *OPPOSITE PAGE*
Sauterne and cream are the perfect accompaniments for Hot Grilled Figs on a Raspberry Pond, served here peeled and scored so that they open like rare autumn flowers (this page).

A Platter of·Figs, Grapes and Walnuts

Serves 4

cluster of grape leaves
8 ripe figs
185 g green grapes
12 unshelled walnuts
chocolate Swiss wafers

This is an idea rather than a recipe for the time of year when fat, ripe figs appear in the shops tasting of late summer sun, sweet grapes arrive around vintage time and fresh walnuts become abundant. Choose the best of each. Arrange the fruits and nuts beautifully, nestling them on a cluster of grape leaves.

- Arrange the grape leaves on a serving platter.

- Cut the figs into halves to reveal their ripeness. Arrange on the platter.

- Rinse the grapes and separate into several small bunches. Place near the figs.

- Arrange the walnuts on the platter, and put out a nut cracker.

- Fan some wafers on one side of the platter.

Banana and Passionfruit Soufflé

Serves 4

2 large *or* 3 small ripe bananas
1 tablespoon lemon juice
1 tablespoon brown rum
4 passionfruit
4 large egg whites
5 tablespoons castor sugar
icing sugar

A very easy puffed fruit soufflé with a fresh flavour, this dish should be taken to the table quickly as it is fragile. Serve with cream or vanilla ice cream.

- Grease a 5-cup soufflé dish.

- Chop the bananas roughly and place in a blender or food processor with the lemon juice and rum, and blend to a purée.

- Put the juice of 2 passionfruit through a sieve into the purée and add the remaining 2 passionfruit including their seeds.

- Beat the whites until stiff, gradually add the castor sugar and beat until a meringue forms.

- Fold one-third of the meringue into the purée, and then the remainder.

- Preheat the oven to 180°C. Pour the mixture into the soufflé dish, place in the centre of the oven and bake for 20 minutes or until firm on top.

- Sift a little icing sugar to frost the top of the soufflé.

Bananas in Sultana and Rum Sauce

Serves 4

60 g sultanas
¼ cup brown rum
3 tablespoons golden syrup
3 tablespoons lemon juice
45 g unsalted butter
4 firm bananas

Brandy can be used instead of rum in this dessert, although the aroma of rum has a particular affinity with bananas. Liqueur would be too sweet in this dish.

- Put the sultanas, rum, golden syrup, lemon juice and butter into a small saucepan and cook until the mixture has come to the boil and the butter melted.

- Peel the bananas and cut into halves lengthwise. Place in a shallow ovenproof dish.

- Pour the sauce over the top of the banana and cover with a lid or foil.

- Preheat the oven to 180°C. Bake the banana for 12 to 15 minutes or until softened.

- Serve plain or with some vanilla ice cream.

Lemon Mascarpone

Serves 6

250 g mascarpone cheese
grated rind of 1 large orange
grated rind of ½ lemon
¼ cup orange juice
¼ cup lemon juice
2 tablespoons castor sugar
a little ground cinnamon

Mascarpone can be a heavy dense dish. Even the Italian classic tirami-su, despite its popularity, makes a rather rich finish for any dinner. However, lightened with fruit juices, mascarpone is quite a different thing altogether. It makes your taste buds tingle with freshness. Pour the mascarpone over fresh berries, or serve in small wine glasses and accompany with almond biscuits. It can be kept, tightly covered, in the refrigerator for 24 hours.

- Beat the cheese for a moment with a fork to soften it. Add all the remaining ingredients except the cinnamon, and mix.

- Taste the mixture. You may find you would like a little more sugar if the lemon was very acidic; or a little more lemon, as the tartness of lemons can vary considerably.

- Pour the mixture into dishes or wine glasses and chill.

- Dust just a whisper of cinnamon (not so much that it takes away from the freshness of the mascarpone) on top of each dish or wine glass before serving.

Mango Slices in Champagne

3 mangoes (about 250 g each)
2 tablespoons orange liqueur
2 tablespoons castor sugar
1 cup chilled champagne
extra chilled champagne

Fruit in champagne always sounds romantic and exciting but can be disappointing, as champagne brings out any acidic or sharp flavours in the fruit. It is more successful if a sugar syrup is made and then freshened with a sparkle of extra champagne before serving. You should be drinking the rest of the bottle with the dish, therefore choose something suitably marvellous to create an occasion.

- Refrigerate the mangoes until ready to serve.

- Put the liqueur into a basin with the castor sugar and champagne, and stir to soften the sugar. Refrigerate.

- Close to serving, cut the skin of each mango to divide into half, peel the skin from one side and cut the flesh into slices. Place in saucer-shaped champagne glasses. The equivalent of half a mango should be sufficient per serve.

- Turn each remaining mango half over. Peel and cut into slices. This is the easiest way to handle mangoes as by leaving the skin on you can grip the fruit. Add the mango to the glasses. The fruit can be served immediately or covered and then refrigerated for 1 hour.

- Pour the chilled liquid over the mango and top with just a little extra chilled champagne.

- Serve while the champagne is still bubbling in the glasses.

Nutmeg Mousse

2 teaspoons gelatine
2 tablespoons water
2 large eggs
⅓ cup sugar
1 tablespoon brandy
1 tablespoon lemon juice
½ teaspoon freshly grated nutmeg
½ teaspoon vanilla essence
½ cup cream

You will not find the taste of raw egg in this dessert, even though it needs no cooking. The flavour is of spicy nutmeg and lemon juice. As the nutmeg is such an important base, grate it fresh if possible for the best of all flavours. The mousse is delicious on its own or with sliced pear or poached prunes.

- Put the gelatine into a cup and add the water. Stir. Stand the cup in a saucepan containing hot water until the gelatine has dissolved.

- With an electric mixer, beat the eggs and sugar until very thick and fluffy.

- Mix the brandy and lemon juice into the dissolved gelatine and then add to the beaten egg. Beat well for 30 seconds.

- Add the nutmeg and vanilla essence.

- Whip the cream until it holds soft peaks. Fold through the mixture and pour into a large bowl or small individual dishes. The mousse sets quite quickly, so you can eat it about an hour after it is made. It can be kept, covered, in the refrigerator for 24 hours.

Orange Gratin

Serves 4

4 large oranges
2 tablespoons orange-flavoured
  liqueur
1 cup thick cream
castor sugar

Oranges are used in this recipe, but a gratin can be made with a number of fruits. Strawberries or raspberries are tart and superb in this dish, giving a marbled pink layer through the cream; ripe nectarines cut into slices are good, as are, of course, ripe white or yellow peaches. Allow about 125 g of berry fruit or 1 large nectarine or peach per person.

- Cut the top and base from each orange and with a sharp knife trim away the skin and all the white pith. Cut each orange into halves. Place, flat side down, on a board and cut into thin slices. Flick out any pips.

- Arrange the orange slices in a shallow ovenproof 20-cm china or glass dish. Pour the liqueur over the top.

- Whisk the cream until it holds soft peaks.

- Spread the cream in a layer over the fruit, taking care not to damage the slices. The cream will only form a thin coating.

- Refrigerate for about 20 minutes.

- Preheat the grill and sift sufficient castor sugar on top of the cream to give a thin but even coating.

- Grill until the top has melted. It will not be even; the effect is of a marbled layer of caramel as the sugar and cream heat and melt.

- Leave to rest for 1 minute before serving.

NOTE Individual gratin dishes are even easier for serving and the flavour is nicer, as the sugar will form little golden bits on the edges. Place them on a flat baking tray under the grill so you can get them out easily, and turn or change their position if they are not browning evenly.

Grilled Pears with Rum

Serves 4

4 ripe pears
45 g unsalted butter
2 tablespoons brown sugar
2 tablespoons brown rum

The pears are not actually cooked in this dish so choose ripe ones. By the time they are piping hot they will be tender and tasting slightly of caramel.

- Peel the pears, core them, and cut into slices.

- Place the pear in a shallow casserole dish.

- Cut the butter into small pieces and dot on top of the pear.

- Scatter the brown sugar on top of the pear, and grill for about 5 minutes or until the pear is hot and coated with syrup.

- Sprinkle rum on top of the pear and shake the dish from side to side so it coats the fruit. Leave to rest for 1 minute.

- Serve plain or with some vanilla ice cream.

Pear with Ginger Syllabub
Serves 4

½ cup thick cream
2 tablespoons castor sugar
1 tablespoon lemon juice
2 tablespoons finely chopped glacé
  ginger
pinch of ground ginger
pinch of ground nutmeg
3 tablespoons dry white wine
4 ripe pears

Light despite the lashings of cream that form its base, syllabub is one of the best of old English desserts. It was originally made by milking the cow directly into a bowl containing alcohol, whereupon a frothy brew formed. It is now made with whipped cream and a little wine and lemon to give a sharp, fresh flavour.

- Whip the cream until it holds stiff peaks.

- Mix the castor sugar with the lemon juice, glacé ginger, ground ginger, nutmeg and wine, and stir to soften the sugar.

- Gradually whisk the mixture into the cream. It should form soft peaks.

- Peel and core the pears and cut them into slices or dice. Place in four individual dishes.

- Spoon the ginger syllabub over the top of the pear and serve immediately.

NOTE The syllabub can be kept refrigerated for about 4 hours, then it tends to separate.

Pears in Passionfruit Sauce
Serves 4

⅓ cup sugar
1 cup water
8 strips orange rind
½ cup freshly squeezed orange
  juice
4 pears
¼ cup thick cream
3 passionfruit

Autumn gives an abundance of passionfruit. Tangy and full of juice, they combine well with the fullness of autumn pears. Buy ripe pears so they cook quickly and give the sauce lots of lush juice.

- Put the sugar, water, orange rind and juice into a saucepan and heat.

- Peel the pears and core them. Halve and quarter. Cut again into a further section so you have eight pieces from each pear.

- Add the pear to the hot syrup and cook without a lid until just tender.

- Add the cream and cook rapidly until slightly thickened. If any of the pear pieces become too soft, remove to a basin.

- Remove the pan from the heat, add the passionfruit pulp, and shake so it mixes through.

- Leave to rest for 5 minutes.

- Serve warm but not hot. You can remove the orange rind or leave it in. Sometimes it will not be soft enough to leave in, so taste a little bit to check.

NOTE This dish is not one to serve chilled. The cream will set and the taste will be heavy, so if you make it in advance reheat gently before serving.

Baked Strawberries with Almonds

Serves 4

2 tablespoons slivered almonds
½ cup apricot jam
2 tablespoons brandy
1 tablespoon brown sugar
2 punnets (500 g) strawberries

Be sure to use sweet ripe strawberries for a baked dish as the cooking brings out their acidity.

- Preheat the oven to 180°C. Put the slivered almonds on an oven try and bake until golden brown. Remove and cool.

- Put the apricot jam, brandy and brown sugar in a small saucepan and heat until bubbling.

- Hull the berries and if large cut into halves. Place in a double layer in a shallow ovenproof dish, and pour the jam mixture through a sieve over the top as evenly as you can.

- Top the strawberries with the toasted almond and bake in the oven until the fruit is heated through and the sauce bubbling. It should take about 8 minutes.

NOTE Be careful not to leave the strawberries in the oven once ready, as long cooking will soften the fruit and make the dish very acidic.

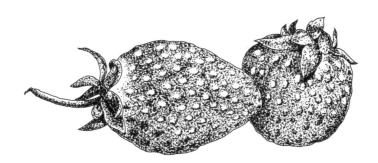

WINTER

Winter is a time to allow yourself a few indulgences and for nostalgic cooking, but it doesn't necessarily mean spending hours in the kitchen. Pork, corned beef and bubbling curries fill the house with appetising aromas, while heartier desserts make a welcome comeback. The range of produce is not as great as in some other seasons; however, root vegetables have a great sweetness and full flavour lacking at other times of the year.

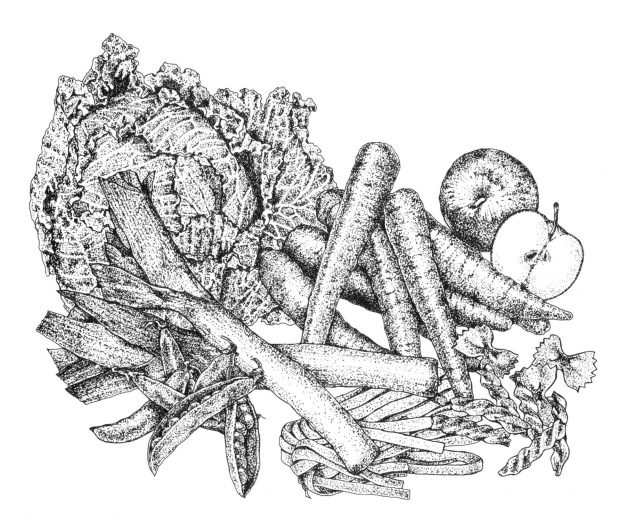

Eggs New Orleans

Serves 4

45 g butter
1 onion, finely chopped
125 g mushrooms, cut into thin
  slices
125 g chopped ham
2 teaspoons plain flour
½ cup dry red wine
salt
pepper
8 eggs
4 tablespoons thick cream

One of the most interesting and food-conscious cities in the United States is New Orleans, where the cooking has a French influence mingled with the spiciness of Spain, a legacy from the years of Spanish domination. While you can eat brunch in most American cities, in New Orleans it is a local institution. The brunch menus feature soups, oysters, baby quail and exotic egg dishes.

Apart from the more familiar egg dishes such as Eggs Benedict, Eggs Florentine and omelettes, most New Orleans restaurants have developed specialities of their own. This dish is not from one particular restaurant but rather reflects the exotic style of New Orleans brunch egg dishes. It can be served for brunch, lunch or as a first course.

- Melt the butter in a frying pan, add the onion and cook until it has softened and has some tinges of gold.

- Add the mushroom and ham and toss for 1 to 2 minutes over a high heat.

- Scatter the flour into the pan. Add the wine and stir until it comes to the boil and thickens. Leave to cook until there is only a little liquid around the mushroom. Season.

- Divide the mushroom mixture between four individual ovenproof casserole dishes or 1-cup gratin dishes.

- Break 2 eggs on top of each dish.

- Trickle a little cream on the eggs and cover the dishes with foil.

- Preheat the oven to 180°C. Cook the eggs for about 15 minutes or until they have just set. Be very careful that they do not become hard.

- Serve in the dishes in which they were cooked, with plenty of hot wholemeal toast.

Crustless Spinach and Cheese Quiche

Serves 4

1 × 250-g packet frozen spinach
100 g bacon, rind removed
30 g butter
1 onion, finely chopped
4 large eggs
1 cup thick cream
2 tablespoons grated Parmesan
  cheese
60 g grated St Claire *or* Jarlsberg
  cheese
salt
pepper
1 ripe tomato, finely sliced

Technically this light, tasty dish cannot really be called a quiche. It is more a savoury custard but is cooked in a quiche dish and has the same texture as a quiche filling. Cook it in a dish that can be taken to the table, and cut the quiche into thin slices. It is fragile without a base so careful lifting is required to keep the slices intact.

- Grease a 20-cm quiche dish.

- Put the spinach into a saucepan, cover, and cook gently until hot. Drain and leave in a sieve.

- While the spinach is cooking, cut the bacon into strips and cook in a dry frying pan until crisp. Drain on kitchen paper.

- Add the butter to the same pan. Add the onion and cook until limp. Return the bacon to the pan along with the spinach, and cook for a couple of minutes.

- Beat the eggs in a basin. Add the cream, both types of cheese, salt and pepper. Stir through the spinach mixture.

- Preheat the oven to 180°C. Pour the mixture into the quiche dish. Bake for about 20 minutes.

- Remove the dish from the oven and arrange the tomato slices on top. Bake for a further 5 to 10 minutes or until the filling is firm and the tomato hot. Leave to rest for 5 minutes before cutting.

Marinated Sardines

Serves 4

400 g canned sardines, drained
1 small onion, finely chopped
¾ cup light olive oil
¼ cup white wine vinegar
salt
pepper
2 teaspoons sugar
2 large hard-boiled eggs, finely
  chopped
3 tablespoons finely chopped fresh
  parsley

Canned sardines are generally reserved for a quick snack, a salad or for mashing and spreading on bread. However, marinating the fish adds a great deal to the flavour and lifts it into a different class. If you have a can of sardines in the pantry this is an ideal quick dish to whip up as a first course in an emergency. It can be served within 5 minutes but will be even better for being left an hour. Serve with crusty brown bread or hot toast.

- Put the sardines on a plate that has a slight edge (for the marinade).

- Place the onion, oil, vinegar, salt, pepper and sugar in a saucepan and simmer gently for 3 minutes.

- Pour the mixture over the sardines and leave to cool. There will be a lot of liquid but some will be absorbed.

- Transfer the fish to a serving platter and spoon a little marinade on top to moisten.

- Scatter the egg on top of the sardines and then put the parsley over the egg.

Rose-tinted Trout Pâté

Serves 4

185 g smoked trout
90 g canned pimentos, drained
freshly ground black pepper
2–3 teaspoons lemon juice
60 g unsalted softened butter
1 tablespoon mayonnaise

The pimento gives the trout a pinky tinge and a smoky flavour. I buy the Spanish type, available in small cans from gourmet shops. The capsicums in jars do not seem to have the same barbecued, smoky flavour but would substitute, if necessary, as long as they are not pickled. An alternative is to grill some capsicums yourself, remove the blackened skin, and use.

I serve this pâté with toast fingers or thin slices of French stick. If you are really in a hurry, use very thin, crisp salt-free biscuits (trout is usually salty).

- Remove any skin and bones from the fish.

- Cut the pimento into a few pieces. Put into a blender or food processor with the trout, and blend.

- Add a little pepper and the lemon juice, and blend again.

- Chop the butter into small pieces and add with the mayonnaise to the mixture. Blend again. Taste and add a little more lemon juice or mayonnaise as required. Usually the trout is quite salty enough, so be cautious about adding any salt.

- Pack the mixture into a crock and refrigerate for 10 minutes, or cover and refrigerate for 24 hours. It is best to remove the pâté from the refrigerator 30 minutes before serving so it is not too hard.

Chicken Livers Bettina

Serves 4

125 g bacon, finely chopped
60 g butter
1 onion, finely chopped
125 g mushrooms
1 large ripe tomato
300 g chicken livers
salt
pepper
1 tablespoon finely chopped fresh
  parsley
1 teaspoon finely chopped fresh
  thyme

This is a rich dish bursting with flavour. Serve just a little with some toast fingers or a small portion of rice as a first course or lunch dish.

- Cook the bacon in a frying pan, stirring occasionally, until the fat is transparent and the bacon crisp.

- Add half the butter and the onion, and cook gently for a few minutes or until slightly softened.

- While the bacon and onion are cooking, cut the mushroom stalks level with the caps and slice the mushrooms thinly. Add to the pan.

- Dice the tomato and mix into the mushroom. Cook for about 5 minutes. Transfer all the vegetables to a bowl.

- Add the remaining half of the butter and the livers to the pan. Cook until the livers have changed colour on the outside. Return the vegetables to the pan and cook gently for a couple of minutes. Season and add the parsley and thyme. Be sure not to over-cook the livers. They should be slightly pink inside, brown on the outside, and surrounded by a thick sauce.

Duck Livers with Hot Vinaigrette Sauce

Serves 4

12 small spinach leaves
8–12 duck livers (depending on
  their size)
90 g butter
2 tablespoons finely chopped
  shallot
2 tablespoons red wine vinegar
salt
pepper
2 tablespoons finely chopped fresh
  chives

The most exotic breakfast I have ever eaten was in San Francisco. The chef and the president of the hotel where I was staying invited me to try one of the specialities of the house, Duck Livers with Hot Vinaigrette Sauce. We began the breakfast with orange juice then went on to try the duck livers with a bottle of champagne and finished by dunking big ripe strawberries into a mixture of sour cream and sugar.

The duck liver dish can be a first course: it is rather rich, even though the vinegar counteracts this somewhat, and is best eaten in small portions. Buy firm plump livers from a good poultry shop. If duck livers are unavailable, substitute chicken livers, but the result will not be the same.

- Remove the tough stalks from the spinach and wash it well. Refrigerate.

- Trim the livers of any veins. Rinse and pat dry.

- Melt half the butter in a frying pan, add the shallot and cook, stirring, for 1 minute.

- Add the livers to the pan. Cook, turning them over, until they are brown on the outside but pink inside.

- Cut the remaining butter into several pieces and add to the pan. Shake the pan so the butter melts quickly. Pour in the vinegar, season with salt and pepper and add the chives.

- Arrange the spinach leaves, overlapping, on individual plates.

- Stir the sauce gently, and spoon the livers and sauce onto the spinach.

Mushrooms with Cream and Parsley

Serves 4

500 g mushrooms
45 g butter
salt
pepper
2 tablespoons cream
2 tablespoons finely chopped fresh
 parsley
1 teaspoon lemon juice

The best flavour of mushrooms is next to the skin so do not peel them or you will lose much of this, and it is not necessary to wash them. If they look a bit dirty, wipe the tops with some damp kitchen paper. Mushrooms absorb water like a sponge and expel this quickly as they are heated, filling the pan with moisture. If you want firm but light-flavoured mushrooms use small button caps, but for a big full flavour select open mushrooms with deep brown gills.

- Cut the stalks of the mushrooms level with the caps.

- Melt the butter in a large frying pan. Add the mushrooms and toss over a high heat.

- Season with salt and pepper once the mushrooms are limp, and keep the heat high so the mushrooms fry rather than stew.

- When the mushrooms have absorbed all the butter add the cream. Cook, still over a high heat, until the mushrooms are just softened.

- Add the parsley and lemon juice, and stir. Serve immediately with hot toast fingers.

NOTE If the mushrooms give out lots of liquid in the pan, before adding the cream keep cooking until it reduces to a thick syrup.

Pea and Curried Potato Soup

Serves 4

2 cups fresh *or* frozen peas
2 cups water *or* chicken stock
1½ cups dry white wine
salt
pepper
30 g butter
1 onion, finely chopped
2–3 teaspoons curry powder
2 large potatoes, cut into dice
1 cup water
a little extra stock *or* milk

This is a really hearty soup with interesting flavours. Some greengrocers sell peas already shelled, which saves time. If these are unobtainable, try frozen peas or dehydrated peas, known as 'surprise peas'.

- Put the peas into a saucepan with the water, stock, wine and salt and pepper to taste. Cook, covered, for about 15 minutes or until the peas are tender.

- While the peas are cooking, melt the butter in a saucepan and add the onion. Stir until slightly wilted. Add the curry powder and leave to fry for 1 minute.

- Add the potato to the pan. Turn it over until it has picked up the colours of the curry. Add the water and cook, covered, for about 10 minutes or until the potato is cooked.

- Purée the pea mixture in a blender or food processor.

- Mix the purée into the potato mixture and stir. Adjust the seasoning and thickness of the soup. A little extra stock or milk can be added.

Spicy Bean Soup

Serves 4

2 tablespoons virgin olive oil
1 onion, chopped
½ teaspoon chilli paste *or* chopped
   chilli
1 cup bottled tomato pasta sauce
3 cups chicken stock
1 × 450-g can kidney beans
¼ cup freshly chopped parsley
¼ cup grated Parmesan cheese

This hearty, nourishing soup is what I would call a total cheat, taking about 5 minutes to make and using commercial products. However, by the time all the ingredients have been combined the flavour is good. Select a tomato pasta sauce that appeals to your taste and has a pure tomato flavour; avoid the ones that contain other flavourings such as bacon, capsicum and mushroom. (See colour plate opposite.)

● Heat the oil in a saucepan and add the onion. Cook for a few minutes or until softened. Add the chilli paste, tomato pasta sauce and stock. Leave to cook for 3 minutes.

● Drain the beans, rinse them in a sieve with cold water, and leave to drain for 1 minute. Add to the soup and reheat.

● Scatter the parsley and cheese on top of the soup, or put a little on top of each serving when serving immediately.

OPPOSITE PAGE ▶
Spicy Bean Soup is a hearty, easy-to-prepare winter first course (this page).

MAIN COURSES

Beef Isabella

Serves 6

2 tablespoons olive oil
2 cloves garlic, chopped
1 cup dry red wine
4 tomatoes, roughly chopped
1 teaspoon green peppercorns,
  drained
1 teaspoon sugar
salt
pepper
1 × 1.5-kg fillet of beef
a little extra olive oil
¼ cup cream

A dish for a special dinner party, Beef Isabella is beef cooked in a red wine and tomato sauce, and the flavours of both linger on the outside of the beef. Braised in a pan, it is beautifully pink and especially moist. Make the sauce first so it will be ready by the time you trim the beef. (See colour plate opposite.)

- Heat the oil in a saucepan, add the garlic and fry gently for a few minutes. Add the red wine and bring to the boil.

- Add the tomato to the pan and cook over a high heat for about 5 minutes.

- Remove the pan from the heat and blend the contents in a blender or food processor. If you find bits of skin, which can happen if the tomatoes are very tough-skinned, you can push the sauce quickly through a sieve.

- Add the peppercorns, sugar, salt and pepper to the blended mixture.

- While the sauce is cooking, trim the beef by removing any fat and sinew from the outside.

- Brown the outside of the meat in a little oil and then transfer to an ovenproof casserole dish, preferably with a lid. If there is no lid, substitute with a double thickness of foil.

- Preheat the oven to 200°C. Pour the hot sauce over the top of the beef and bake for 5 minutes. Turn the oven down to 180°C and cook for about 20 minutes. The timing will depend on the thickness of the fillet and the kind of casserole dish you use.

- Remove the meat from the oven and leave to rest for 5 minutes before carving.

- Either transfer the sauce to a saucepan or if your casserole dish can be put on the stove leave it in this. Pour the cream into the sauce.

- Warm the sauce through again and spoon a little over each slice of beef, or serve the sauce in a jug on the table.

◄   *OPPOSITE PAGE*
Beef Isabella is cooked in a red wine and tomato sauce that is served with the meat (this page). Crispy Zucchini Strips (page 146) and Potatoes Lyonnaise (page 140) complement this rich dish, while a cherry tomato adds colour and freshness.

Fillet Steak with Red Wine Sauce

Serves 4

4 thick pieces fillet steak
a little light olive oil

SAUCE
1 small white onion, very finely
  chopped
45 g butter
½ cup dry red wine
salt
pepper
1 clove garlic, crushed
2 tablespoons finely chopped fresh
  parsley
45 g extra butter

*There is only a small amount of sauce in this dish but it is
intense.*

- Trim the fillet steak of any fat or sinew.

- Press down gently on the meat to flatten slightly.

- Heat a frying pan. Brush the base with the light olive oil and
  when it is smoking add the steak and cook on both sides
  until crusty. Each side should take only a couple of minutes.

- Remove the steaks to a warm plate and put another plate on
  top to keep in the warmth and juices.

- To make the Sauce, wipe out the pan and add the onion and
  butter. Fry, stirring, for a moment. Pour in the red wine and
  add the salt, pepper and garlic. Turn up the heat and cook
  for 1 minute or until the sauce has reduced slightly.

- Add the parsley and butter to the pan, and stir. Remove
  from the heat. The butter will melt and glaze the sauce.

- Return the steaks to the sauce. Turn them over so both sides
  are shiny, and serve with a spoonful of sauce on top.

Roasted Pepper Steak

Serves 4

1 thick piece rump steak
  (750 g–1 kg)
a little light olive oil
1 tablespoon green peppercorns,
  drained
2 tablespoons Dijon mustard
freshly ground black pepper

PIMENTO AND ONION TOPPING
3 large onions
45 g butter
1 tablespoon light olive oil
200 g canned pimentos, drained
salt
pepper

A big thick piece of rump steak roasted in the oven is a marvellous hearty dish and, if you have guests, much easier to cope with than lots of steaks cooking in a pan. Timing depends not on weight but on the thickness of the steak. This dish is covered with pepper, which forms a hot, crusty outside coating. The topping of pimento and onion adds further flavour and colour.

- Preheat the oven to 200°C and place a shallow metal baking dish in it to heat.

- Trim away any fat or sinew from the steak and brush lightly with oil all over.

- Crush the green peppercorns lightly and spread in a layer on one side of the meat.

- Spread a layer of mustard over the peppercorns.

- Coarsely grind the black pepper over the meat to lightly coat.

- Place the meat in the baking dish and bake for about 25 minutes for a weight of 750 g; 35 minutes for 1 kg.

- Remove the meat from the oven and cover with foil. Leave to rest for 10 minutes and then cut into thin slices. Place them, overlapping, on warm plates.

- To make the Pimento and Onion Topping, peel the onions and cut into halves. Place them, cut side down, on a board and cut into thin slices.

- Heat the butter and oil and cook the onion, stirring occasionally, until softened and golden.

- Cut the pimentos into small pieces and add to the onion. Season with salt and pepper.

- Serve the steak with the topping.

NOTE Juice may run from the beef after it has rested for 10 minutes. You can pour this into the topping.

Beef with Red Wine and Onion Sauce

Serves 4

4 pieces scotch fillet
2 large onions
2 tablespoons olive oil
2 teaspoons sugar
1 cup dry red wine
½ cup veal stock *or* chicken stock
salt
freshly ground black pepper
a little extra olive oil

Scotch fillet has lots of flavour and is excellent in a dish such as this. You can prepare the same sauce to go with any good grilling steak or, of course, fillet.

- Flatten the steak slightly with your hand.

- Cut the onions into halves and then segments, rather like an apple. These need not be too fine.

- Heat the oil in a frying pan, add the onion and fry, stirring, until slightly limp. Add the sugar and continue cooking until the onion is tinged with golden specks.

- Pour in the wine and stock, season with salt and pepper and boil for a couple of minutes. Place a lid on the pan, turn down to the lowest heat and simmer gently for about 5 minutes or until the onion is very soft.

- Remove the lid from the pan and leave to cook to reduce the liquid to about half.

- Heat a little extra oil in a frying pan and when it is smoking hot add the steaks and cook, turning, until they are brown on the outside and just pink inside. They should take only about 2 to 3 minutes on each side.

- Serve the steak with the sauce on top, dividing the onion as evenly as possible.

NOTE The sauce is meant to be thin. If you feel it is too light, however, just reduce by boiling rapidly before pouring over the meat.

Glazed Corned Beef of Sage's Cottage

Serves 4

500 g sliced cooked corned beef
½ cup bitter orange marmalade
pinch of ground ginger
½ cup freshly squeezed orange
  juice
pepper
1 tablespoon brown sugar

One of Victoria's oldest farmhouses, Sage's Cottage nestles at the end of a bush track among sighing pines and thick jasmine. Hens, pheasants and guinea fowl wander in the grounds, and descendants of the Shorthorn breed of cattle, originally brought to the property in the 1840s, graze in the paddocks.

Run as a restaurant, Sage's Cottage concentrates on Australian colonial cooking, and in those days brined meats featured strongly. You can buy corned beef ready-cooked at delicatessens. Ask for it to be cut thickly.

- Arrange the corned beef in a shallow ovenproof casserole dish.

- Put the remaining ingredients into a saucepan, bring to the boil and pour over the corned beef.

- Preheat the oven to 180°C. Cook the corned beef for about 15 to 20 minutes or until it has heated and the sauce is glazed on top.

Hamburgers with Creamy Onion

Serves 4

45 g butter
250 g onions, cut into thin
  half-slices
½ cup chicken stock
¼ cup cream
salt
pepper
500 g finely minced beef
1 extra teaspoon salt
extra pepper
2 extra tablespoons cream
1 tablespoon light olive oil
4 thick slices country bread, crusts
  removed
French mustard

Adding a little cream to the hamburgers makes them paler in colour but adds a great deal of moistness to the meat. If you would prefer to omit the cream be careful not to over-cook the beef, particularly if it is very lean.

- Melt the butter in a saucepan and add the onion. Cook, stirring occasionally, until the onion is just tinged with gold and a few brown specks here and there.

- Add the stock and the ¼ cup of cream to the pan and season. Cook, covered, until very soft.

- Remove the lid from the pan. Cook until the liquid has mostly reduced and the onion is creamy soft.

- Place the meat in a basin, season with 1 teaspoon of salt, and pepper. Add the 2 tablespoons of cream. Mix well and with damp hands form into four patties.

- Heat the oil in a frying pan. When very hot cook the patties on both sides so they are crusty brown on the outside and still pink inside.

- Toast the bread and cut to the same shape as the hamburgers.

- Spread the toast with French mustard, cover with onion sauce and top with a piece of toast to make a hamburger. Make four hamburgers and serve.

Fillet of Pork with Apple Sauce

Serves 6

3 medium-sized *or* 6 small fillets of
  pork
plain flour
2 eggs
2 tablespoons Dijon mustard
2 teaspoons water
oil

APPLE SAUCE
1 × 450-g can dessert or pie
  pack apple
½ cup dry white wine
2 teaspoons sugar

Fillets of pork can vary considerably in size. If they are medium to large you may find half per person is sufficient; if small ones allow one per person. The coating will seal and flavour the outside of the pork and the apple sauce is tart and exceptionally easy.

- Trim any fat or sinew from the pork, and cut each fillet into halves lengthwise down the centre.

- Put the flour on a piece of greaseproof paper.

- Beat the eggs with the mustard and water in a basin.

- Dust the pork with the flour, shake away the excess, and then dip into the egg and mustard mixture.

- You really need to cook the pork once you do this, as if left to rest the egg mixture will fall away. Heat some oil in a large frying pan and when sizzling add the pork. Cook on one side until golden and turn over and cook on the other side. The pork should not cook so quickly that it browns too much before it is cooked through.

- To make the Apple Sauce, put the apple into a saucepan with the wine and sugar, and cook, uncovered, for about 5 minutes.

- Purée the apple mixture in a blender or food processor and keep warm if serving immediately, or refrigerate and reheat when needed.

- Serve the pork with the sauce on top.

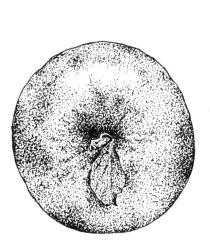
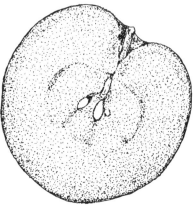

Chicken Breasts with Orange Sauce

Serves 4

4 chicken breasts, boned and
  skinned
seasoned plain flour
45 g butter
½ cup orange juice
grated rind of 1 orange
¼ cup chicken stock
2 teaspoons redcurrant jelly
2 tablespoons flaked almonds

This is an easy dish but be sure not to over-cook the chicken or the breasts will become dry.

- Dust the chicken breasts with the seasoned flour.

- Melt the butter in a frying pan and cook the chicken on both sides until it has changed colour. The breasts will still be raw inside. Transfer to a shallow baking dish in which they fit in one layer.

- Mix all the remaining ingredients, except the almonds, in a basin.

- Wipe out the frying pan, add the orange mixture, bring to the boil and pour over the chicken breasts.

- Preheat the oven to 180°C. Bake the chicken, uncovered, for about 15 minutes or until tender and cooked through.

- While the chicken is cooking, place the flaked almonds on a flat tray and toast for 2 minutes or until golden.

- Place each chicken breast on a plate and top with some sauce and a scattering of flaked almonds.

Devilled Chicken Breasts

Serves 4

4 chicken breasts, boned and
  skinned
45 g butter
2 teaspoons dry English mustard
2 teaspoons French mustard
1 tablespoon Worcestershire sauce
1 tablespoon tomato sauce
1 clove garlic, crushed
salt
breadcrumbs made from stale bread

'Devilled' indicates a hot and fiery sauce. It was once used to make leftover meat more interesting – the meat was cut into pieces, dipped in a devilled sauce, and then crumbed and fried in oil or butter. This recipe uses fresh meat but the principle is the same: a very spicy mixture is spread over chicken before the poultry is coated with crumbs.

- Place some plastic wrap over the chicken breasts. Using a rolling pin flatten them slightly so they are the same thickness.

- Melt the butter in a frying pan, add the breasts and cook gently for about 2 minutes on each side. They will still be raw inside. Place on a greased baking tray.

- Mix all the ingredients, except the breadcrumbs, in a basin. Spread over the chicken to the edges. The mixture will be quite thin on the warm chicken.

- With your hands press on sufficient breadcrumbs to coat the top of the breasts.

- Preheat the oven to 180°C. Bake the chicken for about 10 minutes or until cooked through and the top is brown.

NOTE If the breadcrumbs are still soft place the breasts under the grill for about 2 minutes.

Chicken Breasts Russian Style

Serves 6

6 chicken breasts, boned and
  skinned
45 g butter
250 g mushrooms
1 large clove garlic
2 tablespoons plain flour
2 teaspoons ground sweet paprika
1 tablespoon tomato paste
½ cup dry white wine
1 cup chicken stock
salt
pepper
2 tablespoons finely chopped fresh
  parsley
½ cup sour cream

This creamy, rich dish is made in a similar manner to Beef Stroganoff and, in fact, you can use a good quality beef instead of chicken if you wish. There should be plenty of sauce, which is a little on the runny side and ideal mingled with plain noodles or a buttery pasta dish.

- Cut the chicken breasts into thick strips. You should get about four from each one.

- Melt the butter in a wide, deep frying pan and add the chicken, about half at a time.

- Cook the chicken until it changes colour.

- While the chicken is cooking, slice the mushrooms thickly and chop the garlic.

- Transfer the chicken from the pan to a side plate.

- Add the mushroom to the pan. Cook over a high heat until it has softened.

- Add the garlic to the pan and scatter the flour and paprika on top. Fry for about 30 seconds.

- Add the tomato paste, wine and stock to the pan and, stirring, bring to the boil. Cook for a few minutes until thickened and then return the chicken to the pan. Cook on the lowest heat for about 5 minutes. The chicken will heat and continue cooking gently.

- Just before serving add the parsley and sour cream, reheat and serve.

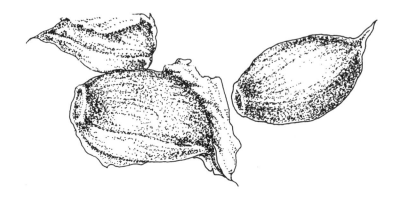

Chicken on a Bed of Peas and Ham   *Serves 4*

2 cups water
45 g butter
1 teaspoon sugar
1 teaspoon salt
2 tablespoons roughly chopped
  fresh parsley
¼ teaspoon ground nutmeg
2 cups frozen peas
2 teaspoons plain flour
¼ cup cream
125 g chopped ham
4 chicken breasts, boned and
  skinned
seasoned plain flour
45 g butter

To save time you can use frozen peas, and the seasonings I have used will spark up their flavour. Some greengrocers now sell peas ready shelled and if they are young and sweet then, of course, they are even better. The only difference will be the cooking time: instead of about 5 minutes for frozen peas you will probably need to allow about 12 minutes for fresh ones.

- Heat the water with the butter, sugar, salt, parsley and nutmeg. When boiling add the peas and cook for about 5 minutes. Drain, reserving 1 cup of liquid.

- Mix the flour and cream together.

- Return the peas and the 1 cup of reserved liquid to the pan and mix in the flour and cream, stirring until it comes to the boil.

- Add the ham to the pan. Spoon the mixture onto the base of a shallow casserole dish that will fit the chicken breasts in one layer.

- To prepare the chicken, dip the breasts into the seasoned flour.

- Heat the butter in a frying pan and sauté the breasts on both sides until they have changed colour.

- Place the breasts on top of the peas and ham in the casserole dish. Brush the chicken with any butter from the pan.

- Preheat the oven to 180°C. Bake the chicken for about 12 minutes or until cooked. If the peas begin to dry, cover with foil or add a spoonful of hot water to the side of the dish.

- Serve each chicken breast on a bed of peas and ham.

Grilled Spicy Chicken

Serves 6

2 tablespoons vegetable oil
½ mild onion, cut into rough
  pieces
3 cloves garlic
3 slices fresh ginger
2 teaspoons ground coriander
½ teaspoon ground cinnamon
½ teaspoon ground chilli *or*
  1 teaspoon chilli sauce
1 teaspoon salt
½ teaspoon ground cummin
2 tablespoons white wine vinegar
1 tablespoon tomato paste
6 chicken breasts, boned and
  skinned
extra vegetable oil

A thick paste is applied to the chicken breasts, which are then grilled until cooked through. The topping forms a golden coating and keeps the chicken very succulent. You could serve this dish with some rice followed by a green salad.

- In a blender or food processor blend all the ingredients, except the chicken, to a coarse purée.

- Put the chicken breasts on a plate. Paste the chicken with the purée. (It is rather messy but this does not matter.) You can leave it to marinate for 15 minutes or as long as 4 hours.

- Brush a sheet of foil with the oil. Place the chicken on the foil.

- Preheat the grill. Grill the chicken, turning once, until cooked through. Depending on the grill, the first side should take about 5 minutes, the second side 2 to 3 minutes.

NOTE The chicken can be baked in the oven. The colour will not be as interesting but the flavour is very good. It takes about 12 to 15 minutes.

Chicken with Pimento and Onion

Serves 4

1.5 kg chicken portions (such as
  drumsticks, thighs, wings, pieces
  of breast on the bone)
30 g butter
1 tablespoon light olive oil
salt
pepper
1 onion, finely chopped
125 g canned pimentos, drained
  and chopped
1 clove garlic, crushed
½ cup chicken stock
3 tablespoons sour cream
1 tablespoon horseradish relish
1 tablespoon finely chopped fresh
  parsley

Available in delicatessens and the gourmet section of supermarkets, pimento is smoky, skinned capsicum, which gives a special flavour to this sauce.

- If the chicken portions vary in weight and size, cut them as evenly as you can so they will cook evenly.

- Melt the butter with the oil in a frying pan. When very hot add the chicken portions and cook until they have changed colour all over.

- Remove the chicken from the pan and season it with salt and pepper.

- Add the onion to the same pan and fry for a couple of minutes or until wilted. Place in an ovenproof casserole dish.

- Scatter the pimento over the onion and top with the chicken portions.

- Preheat the oven to 180°C. Pour the stock over the chicken and bake for about 35 minutes or until the chicken is tender.

- Mix the sour cream with the horseradish, and spoon over the cooked chicken. Leave for a minute (the dish will be hot enough so do not return it to the oven).

- Scatter the parsley over the chicken and serve.

Fragrant Chicken Curry

Serves 4

8 boned drumsticks *or* 4 chicken breasts
80 g butter
1 large onion, roughly chopped
500 g ripe tomatoes, roughly chopped
salt
pepper
1 teaspoon sugar
2 teaspoons finely chopped *or* grated fresh ginger
1 tablespoon curry powder
¼ cup sprigs coriander

Cooked fresh tomatoes are puréed to give a light pink sauce, which coats the chicken. Boned drumsticks, sold at good poultry shops, are particularly succulent and reheat well. If these are unobtainable use chicken breasts, but be careful not to over-cook or they can become dry. Serve with plain boiled or steamed rice, some mango chutney and a dish of toasted coconut.

- Cut the drumsticks into halves or each chicken breast into four strips lengthwise.

- Melt 45 g of the butter in a saucepan, add the onion and cook gently until it is limp and tinged with gold.

- Put the tomato into a saucepan and cook over a moderate heat until it is a reasonably thick sauce. Stir occasionally and season with salt and pepper and, if not sweet, add the sugar.

- Push the tomato through a sieve over the top of the onion, pressing down to get out all the juices. Leave this mixture to simmer for 1 minute.

- Melt the remaining butter in a frying pan, add the ginger and fry for 30 seconds. Add the chicken and cook until it has changed colour on the outside.

- Scatter the curry powder on the chicken. Leave to fry for 1 minute or until aromatic, and then pour the onion and tomato on top.

- Cook the chicken gently in the sauce until tender. It should take about 5 minutes. Add the coriander sprigs, and serve.

Spiced Chicken Wings
Serves 4

1 kg chicken wings
2 tablespoons peanut oil
2 tablespoons soy sauce
2 tablespoons tomato sauce
¼ cup honey
1 small clove garlic, crushed
¼ teaspoon five-spice powder
¼ teaspoon salt

Buy entire wings and not just the end of the wings if you can. It is the portion nearest the bird that is the most succulent.

- Remove the wing tips.

- Mix all the remaining ingredients in a large basin and add the chicken wings. Stir to coat with the sauce.

- Place the wings in a flat shallow dish so they fit in one layer.

- Preheat the oven to 180°C. Cook the wings for about 45 minutes, turning them over once so they cook evenly. If they become too brown reduce the heat and, if dry, add 1 tablespoon of water. When ready the outside should be sticky and caramelised and the inside very soft and tender so the chicken almost falls away from the bone.

NOTE If you can only buy small chicken wings, or the end of the wings, they will not need such long cooking. About 30 minutes should be sufficient.

Split Chicken with Sesame Seeds
Serves 4

2 small chickens (about 1.25 kg
  each)
2 tablespoons vegetable oil
2 tablespoons lemon juice
1 clove garlic, crushed
salt
pepper
2 tablespoons honey
2 tablespoons toasted sesame seeds

For easy serving use small chickens and cut each one in half through the centre of the breast; larger chickens need to be cut into four and require an additional 20 minutes.

- Cut alongside the backbone of the chicken. Remove any fat, and press down to flatten.

- Brush a shallow baking dish with half the oil. Put the chickens, side by side with the breast upwards, into the dish.

- Mix the remaining oil with the lemon juice and garlic and brush over the top of the chickens. Season.

- Preheat the oven to 180°C. Bake the chickens for about 30 minutes or until almost cooked.

- Remove the chickens from the oven. Brush or trickle the honey over the chickens and scatter sesame seeds on top (they will stick to the honey).

- Bake the chickens for a further 10 minutes or until the top is golden and glazed. Leave to rest for 5 minutes.

- Cut each chicken through the centre of the breast and serve half a chicken per person.

Rice with Peas and Bacon

Serves 4

2 tablespoons oil
1 onion, roughly chopped
125 g bacon, cut into strips
1½ cups long-grain rice
3 cups chicken stock *or* water
1 cup peas
salt
pepper
30 g butter

You can use fresh or frozen peas in this dish; fresh peas are only better if they are young and sweet. A good accompaniment to chicken or spicy food, the dish also makes a light lunch dish on its own.

- Heat the oil in a saucepan. Add the onion and fry, stirring, for 1 minute.

- Add the bacon and cook until the bacon fat is transparent.

- Add the rice and stir. Cook until the rice grains have become opaque and then add the stock. Bring to the boil and add the peas. Season, according to the stock, and put a tight-fitting lid on the pan. Let it cook over a gentle heat for about 20 minutes. The rice grains should be tender and the liquid absorbed. Avoid lifting the lid to keep checking or you will let out the steam.

- When the rice is ready, add the butter, leave to melt, and fluff up the rice with two forks.

Rice Pilaf

Serves 4

2 tablespoons peanut oil *or* light olive oil
1½ cups long-grain rice
3 cups chicken stock
salt
pepper
30 g butter

This is perfect as a side dish for curry or served with a variety of vegetables for a light meatless meal. Always use long-grain rice: basmati, one of the best varieties of rice grown, has a wonderful fragrance and flavour.

- Heat the oil in a heavy-based saucepan and add the rice. Cook, stirring, until it has become opaque in parts.

- Add the stock, salt and pepper and bring to the boil.

- Place a lid on top, turn the heat down to very low and cook for about 20 minutes or until the rice is tender and the liquid absorbed. Avoid lifting the lid to keep checking or you will let out the steam. Check after about 16 minutes if not sure.

- Add the butter, push into the centre of the rice so it will melt, and then toss with two forks.

NOTE If serving with a very plain dish add ⅓ cup of grated Parmesan cheese along with the butter for an enhanced flavour.

Luciano's Midnight Pasta

Serves 4

1 tablespoon salt
1 tablespoon oil
375 g fine spaghetti
½ cup virgin olive oil
1 small chilli
2 large cloves garlic, crushed
3 tablespoons finely chopped fresh
  parsley
½ cup freshly grated Parmesan
  cheese

Lake Como is one of the loveliest parts of Italy's lake district, its villas and towns steeped in history and legend. On the shores of Como, near the tiny village of Cernobbio, is the luxury hotel the Villa d'Este with a history dating back to the sixteenth century. The cooking of this hotel remains distinctly Italian. Chef Luciano Pariolari says that midnight is the only time a true Italian would eat pasta as a main dish. At other times it is a first course. When he has finished work he often whips up a plate of this rich and zesty pasta.

It is only really a success if the oil is a fruity virgin olive oil and the Parmesan has been freshly grated.

- Bring a large saucepan of water to the boil, add the salt, oil and pasta. Cook over a high heat until just tender. Judge by testing a strand between your teeth.

- Heat the virgin olive oil gently in a frying pan.

- Cut the chilli into halves lengthwise and wash out the seeds. Chop the chilli and add to the oil.

- Add the garlic and leave the mixture to warm but do not fry the garlic, as it will become bitter.

- Drain the pasta. Add the garlic mixture to the pasta and toss well.

- Add the parsley and half the cheese to the pasta, and mix. Serve with the remainder of the cheese on the table.

Baked Pasta

Serves 4

185 g small macaroni *or* shell pasta
1 large onion, roughly chopped
3 tablespoons virgin olive oil
250 g zucchini
2 large eggs
¾ cup bottled tomato pasta sauce
125 g St Claire *or* Jarlsberg cheese,
  grated or chopped
generous dash of Tabasco *or* chilli
  sauce
¼ cup cream

The main flavouring of this tasty 'set' pasta dish is a mixture of fresh grated zucchini with tomato sauce. From the wide variety of brands, choose a tomato sauce that you enjoy. I generally use an Italian one that has a very natural flavour.

- Bring a large saucepan of water to the boil, salt well and add the macaroni. Keep bubbling rapidly until just tender. The best way to judge is to taste.

- While the macaroni is cooking, heat the oil in a saucepan, add the onion, and cook until softened.

- Remove the ends from the zucchini and grate it.

- When the onion is wilted add the zucchini and cook for a couple of minutes.

- Put the onion and zucchini in a basin, add the eggs, tomato sauce and cheese.

- Drain the macaroni and leave to cool for 5 minutes.

- Mix the vegetables through the macaroni with the Tabasco and cream. Stir well.

- Grease a shallow 5-cup ovenproof dish and pour in the macaroni mixture. Smooth the top. It can be kept, refrigerated, for 8 hours at this stage or baked immediately.

- Preheat the oven to 180°C. Cook the macaroni mixture for about 20 minutes or until bubbling on the edges and crusty on top. If you have made the dish hours in advance, especially if it has been refrigerated, you will need to add an extra 10 minutes' oven time.

Tagliatelle with Three Cheeses   *Serves 4*

salt
375 g tagliatelle
1 cup grated St Claire *or* Jarlsberg
  cheese
3 tablespoons grated Parmesan
  cheese
1 tablespoon blue cheese
1 cup cream
extra salt
pepper

The first time I visited Rome friends took me to a small but famous restaurant recognised for its antipasto and homemade pasta. The four of us ordered tagliatelle with cheese and the waiter appeared with a huge white oval platter, like a great big meat plate, and three dinner plates. Expertly he served the tagliatelle onto the three plates and then ceremoniously deposited the huge platter in front of me, explaining that the best flavour of all would be on the big platter. You may not want to follow this custom, but the pasta sauce is lovely. Be sure to get good fresh cheese for grating and do it yourself; avoid the pre-grated cheese no matter how busy you are. Avoid serving too large a portion, as it is rich.

- Bring a large saucepan of water to the boil and season with salt. Add the tagliatelle and push it down under the water to soften. Cook until tender and drain.

- Put the three cheeses into a saucepan, add the cream and warm gently until the cheese has melted. Avoid leaving the mixture too long or the St Claire cheese will become stringy.

- Pour over the pasta, stir so the pasta is coated with cheese, and season.

- Serve immediately with some more grated Parmesan on the table.

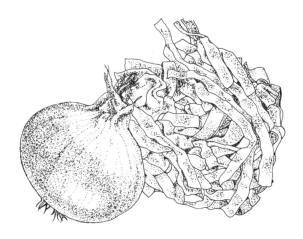

Pasta Casa Mia

Serves 6

salt
375 g fine spaghetti *or* tagliatelle
1 × 220-g can pimentos, drained
2 cups bottled tomato pasta sauce
¾ cup cream
4 rashers bacon, rind removed
2 cloves garlic, crushed *or* finely
  chopped
⅓ cup sprigs parsley, chopped
¾ cup grated Jarlsberg *or* St Claire
  cheese

A glorious reddish colour and a lightly smoked flavour distinguish this sauce. Buy the plainest tomato pasta sauce you can find, without too many additional flavourings or spices. Use the canned Spanish pimentos; avoid using other varieties of canned or bottled capsicums or peppers as some of them contain vinegar, which would ruin the dish. (See colour plate opposite.)

- Bring a large saucepan of water to the boil, salt generously and add the pasta.

- While the pasta is cooking, blend the pimentos in a blender or food processor to a purée.

- Place the purée in a saucepan with the tomato pasta sauce and cook gently until it comes to the boil. Add the cream and bring to the boil. Remove from the heat and keep warm.

- Cut the bacon into dice or strips and fry in a frying pan.

- Mix the garlic and parsley into the bacon and cook for about 2 minutes.

- Drain the pasta as soon as it is ready and place in a large bowl. Pour the tomato and pimento sauce over the top, add the cheese and mix. Scatter the bacon, garlic and parsley on top.

OPPOSITE PAGE ▶
Pimentos, bacon, tomatoes, cheese and cream form the smoky-flavoured base of Pasta Casa Mia (this page).

DESSERTS

Elizabethan Cherries
Serves 8

1 × 820-g can dark cherries
grated rind of 1 orange
piece cinnamon stick
1 generous tablespoon redcurrant
 jelly
1 tablespoon cornflour *or*
 arrowroot
a little water
1 tablespoon brandy
1 tablespoon Grand Marnier *or*
 Cointreau
vanilla ice cream
60 g grated dark chocolate

This is a dish for a time when you feel like cherries but the fresh ones are out of season. A warm dish with a very full flavour, it is served with a scoop of ice cream, which will melt and mingle with the cherry juice. The dish can be prepared and served immediately or reheated when required. (See colour plate opposite.)

- Strain the juice from the cherries into a saucepan. Add the orange rind and cinnamon stick and bring slowly to the boil. Leave to cook gently for about 4 minutes.

- Add the redcurrant jelly to the pan and cook until dissolved.

- Mix the cornflour with the water to make a thin paste. Add to the pan and stir until it comes to the boil.

- Add the cherries to the pan. Let them warm through for a minute in the sauce.

- While the cherries are warming, grate the chocolate coarsely.

- Put a scoop of vanilla ice cream in the centre of each plate or dish. Surround the ice cream with the cherries and sauce, discarding the cinnamon stick, and scatter the chocolate on top.

◀ *OPPOSITE PAGE*
Elizabethan Cherries is a warm dish with a full flavour that suits winter dining (this page).

Aztecs' Delight

3 tablespoons sultanas
⅓ cup roughly chopped pecan
  nuts
2 tablespoons brandy
1 cup sugar
1½ tablespoons cornflour
4 tablespoons cocoa
pinch of salt
1 teaspoon vanilla essence
4 large eggs
1¼ cups cream

Legend has it that every night before entering his harem, Montezuma, the Aztec emperor of Mexico, was served a generous bowl of chocolate to sustain him. It may not be guaranteed to affect virility but this creamy chocolate dessert is deliciously rich and almost fudgey in texture. Lovely straight from the oven, it is just as good at room temperature. Be careful not to cook it for too long as it will become hard. The texture should be soft, so take it from the oven while the middle is a little runny.

- Put the sultanas, nuts and brandy into a basin and leave to marinate.

- Put the sugar into a basin and sift the cornflour, cocoa and salt over the top.

- Add the vanilla essence, eggs and cream to the mixture, and beat for 30 seconds with a wooden spoon.

- Divide the sultana mixture between 6 small soufflé dishes or ramekins.

- Pour the chocolate mixture over the top of the sultana mixture to three-quarter fill the dishes.

- Preheat the oven to 180°C. Bake the dessert for about 20 minutes or until just set on the edges and creamy in the centre. Cool for 5 minutes before serving.

- Serve accompanied by orange segments or vanilla ice cream if you wish.

Apple Baked in Orange Liqueur

Serves 4

45 g unsalted butter
½ cup orange juice
750 g Granny Smith apples
2 tablespoons sugar
3 tablespoons orange-flavoured
  liqueur

At a time of year when fruits are not so plentiful apples are always a blessing and, gently poached in orange liqueur, they become an exotic dessert. Use Grand Marnier, Curaçao or Cointreau, or, if you like to experiment, whisky or bourbon is very good too.

- Put the butter and orange juice into a casserole dish that has a tight-fitting lid.

- Preheat the oven to 180°C. Place the casserole dish in the oven to warm while you prepare the apples.

- Peel, core and slice the apples thickly. Place in the dish.

- Scatter the sugar on top of the apple and add 1 tablespoon of the liqueur. Stir gently so the fruit is moist and return, tightly covered, to the oven.

- Cook the apple for about 25 minutes or until just soft and stir once to be sure it cooks evenly.

- Pour the remaining liqueur over the top of the apple, cover, and leave to rest for 10 minutes before serving. You can serve the apple plain if you want a fresh taste; for a richer flavour put a jug of cream on the table.

Apple Cream

Serves 4

250 g Granny Smith apples
30 g butter
2 tablespoons brown sugar
2 large eggs
1 cup cream
½ teaspoon vanilla essence
1 tablespoon castor sugar
1 tablespoon brandy
a little ground cinnamon

A cross between a set custard and a creamy mixture, this is a lovely winter dessert that could also be prepared in summer with small ripe apricot halves.

- Peel and core the apples and cut them into dice.

- Place the apple in a 3-cup pie dish and scatter bits of butter and the brown sugar over the top.

- Preheat the oven to 180°C. Cook the apple for about 10 to 15 minutes or until slightly softened. Stir once so it cooks evenly.

- Beat the eggs with the cream, vanilla essence, castor sugar and brandy, and pour over the hot apple.

- Continue cooking the apple for another 15 minutes or until the custard is just barely set. Dust with the cinnamon and leave to rest for 5 minutes before serving.

Apple Puff

1 × 450-g can dessert or pie pack
  apple
2 tablespoons cornflour
¼ cup water
1 teaspoon ground cinnamon
1 tablespoon orange marmalade
4 egg whites
4 tablespoons sugar
a little icing sugar

Dessert apples, sometimes called pie pack apples, are available canned. Unsweetened and with a good firm texture, they are ideal to use as a base in this dessert, which is as light as a soufflé and very quick to make. Apple Puff can also be served cold. Once cool this dessert will not be puffed on top but will taste just as delicious.

- Preheat the oven to 180°C and grease a 5-cup soufflé dish.

- Purée the apple in a blender or food processor.

- Place half the purée in a saucepan and put on a low heat to warm through.

- Mix the cornflour with the water and add to the warm apple. Cook, stirring, until the mixture comes to the boil and thickens.

- Stir the hot apple into the reserved apple purée, add the cinnamon and orange marmalade, and mix.

- Beat the egg whites until stiff, add the 4 tablespoons of sugar and beat again until glossy. Fold into the apple, a little at a time.

- Place the mixture into the prepared soufflé dish and bake for about 20 minutes or until firm to touch.

- Sift a little icing sugar over the top of the puff and serve immediately. Put a jug of cream on the table.

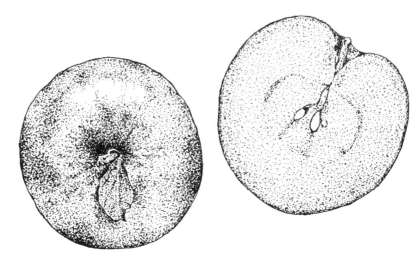

Quick Apricot Dessert Cake

Serves 8

1 × 880-g can apricot halves,
  drained
30 g butter
⅓ cup sugar
½ cup self-raising flour
1 large egg
2 tablespoons milk
1 teaspoon vanilla essence
a little castor sugar mixed with a
  little ground cinnamon

This is an easy cake that could be made using any canned fruits; plums, peaches or drained cherries are all good.

- Place the apricot halves, cut side down, in a greased 20-cm cake dish. If they do not fit exactly, trim a few into quarters.

- Melt the butter in a saucepan.

- While the butter is melting put the sugar and flour into a basin and mix.

- Pour the melted butter into a large cup, add the egg, milk and vanilla essence and beat for a few seconds.

- Tip the contents of the cup into the sugar and flour and beat with a wooden spoon for 1 minute. Dot the mixture across the top of the apricot. There will not be a lot of mixture but it will melt in a layer as it cooks. Spread out as best you can with a knife.

- Preheat the oven to 180°C. Bake the cake for 20 to 25 minutes.

- Remove the cake from the oven and scatter the castor sugar and cinnamon on top while still hot.

- Serve the cake, cut into thick wedges, with some running or lightly whipped cream.

Bananas in Orange Sauce

Serves 4

4 large bananas, peeled
plain flour
45 g unsalted butter
2 tablespoons brown sugar
2 tablespoons white sugar
grated rind of 1 orange
½ cup orange juice
2 tablespoons orange-flavoured
  liqueur

This is the kind of dish that can be put together easily. It is a life-saver if you have unexpected guests – providing you have bananas in your fruit bowl. All the other ingredients are usually found in most pantries. Sweetly citrus flavoured, the sauced bananas can be served on their own or are delicious with vanilla ice cream.

- Dust the bananas lightly with flour.

- Melt the butter in a frying pan, add the bananas and scatter both types of sugar on top. Cook gently so the sugar caramelises, and watch carefully as the bananas tend to stick if left.

- Add the orange rind and juice to the bananas and leave to cook until the sticky bits of caramel have melted.

- Cook the bananas gently until the sauce has slightly thickened, add the liqueur, and serve.

Prunes and Oranges in Orange Syrup

Serves 4

½ cup water
¼ cup castor sugar
grated rind of 1 orange
250 g large prunes
½ cup orange juice
3 oranges
1 tablespoon brown rum *or* brandy

As this dessert is best served cool prepare it at least an hour in advance. If in a hurry you can put it in the freezer for 10 minutes. Prunes are delicious if cooked and prepared in the right manner. They should be soft but not breaking up, and soaked in a fresh syrup. The dish keeps beautifully and, in fact, improves if left for a day or two.

- Put the water, sugar and orange rind into a saucepan, cover, and cook gently for 10 minutes.

- Add the prunes and cook, uncovered, over the lowest heat for about 5 minutes. Add the orange juice and remove to a bowl.

- Peel the oranges, removing all the white pith, and cut into segments. Add to the prunes and mix in the rum. Stir very gently and refrigerate.

Liqueur Soufflé Omelette

Serves 4

4 egg yolks
3 tablespoons castor sugar
3 tablespoons liqueur
30 g unsalted butter
4 egg whites
icing sugar

This is a last-minute dish but one that can be quickly made. Any good liqueur can be used. If the liqueur is very sweet, such as Cointreau, 3 tablespoons of sugar will be plenty; if not so sweet you may like to add an extra tablespoon of liqueur. When making this kind of omelette soufflé a non-stick frying pan is an enormous help.

- Put the egg yolks and castor sugar into a basin and beat until thick. Add 1 tablespoon of the liqueur and mix through.

- Melt the butter in a non-stick frying pan and preheat the grill.

- Beat the egg whites until they hold stiff peaks and gently fold them, a third at a time, into the egg yolk base.

- Pour the egg mixture into the hot butter and smooth to the edges. It should set on the base immediately. Leave to cook over a gentle heat until partly set. It will still be uncooked on top.

- Transfer the omelette to the grill and cook until just firm to touch. Avoid over-cooking or it will become dry. Turn out onto a plate.

- Sift the icing sugar on top of the omelette.

- In a saucepan warm the remaining liqueur, light it, and pour around the base of the omelette.

Chocolate Soufflé Omelette

Serves 4

3 egg yolks
2 tablespoons castor sugar
2 tablespoons cocoa
1 tablespoon brandy
4 egg whites
pinch of salt
1 extra tablespoon castor sugar
15 g unsalted butter
a little icing sugar

This dessert has the fluffy texture and rich chocolate flavour of a soufflé made in the oven, but for speed it is cooked in a non-stick frying pan. Cook gently so it does not catch on the base before the soufflé mixture has begun to cook through. Serve with ice cream or cream trickled with chocolate sauce.

- Place the egg yolks with the castor sugar in a basin.

- Sift the cocoa over the top of the egg yolks and sugar, and beat for 1 minute or until thick.

- Add the brandy to the mixture and stir through.

- Beat the egg whites until they hold stiff peaks. Add the salt and the extra sugar and beat again.

- Gently fold the egg white mixture into the egg yolk mixture, a third at a time.

- Melt the butter in a non-stick frying pan. When very hot gently pour in the chocolate mixture and spread to the edges. Keep the heat medium to low for about 3 to 4 minutes. Turn it down if the bottom begins to look too brown. You can easily check by lifting an edge, which will have set quickly.

- Preheat the grill. Place the pan underneath the grill and cook until the omelette has puffed. Be careful not to leave it for too long or it will become dry.

- Either turn the omelette gently out onto a big plate or serve directly from the pan. Sift the icing sugar on top of the omelette.

NOTE When serving, pull the omelette apart with two forks or a fork and a spoon rather than cutting with a knife, which will compress the edges so the dish will not be as light.

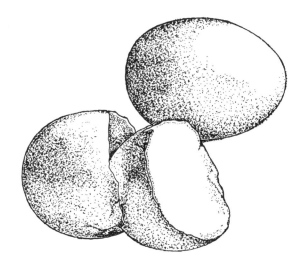

Light Chocolate Pudding

Serves 6

2 cups milk
2 tablespoons castor sugar
6 dried, packeted ladyfingers
100 g dark chocolate, broken into
  pieces
2 eggs
½ teaspoon vanilla essence

The flavour of this dish does not indicate the ease and simplicity of its preparation. Full of chocolate with a lightness on the palate, it can be eaten warm from the oven or left to cool completely and then served chilled.

Buy the dried, packeted ladyfingers, which are easily obtainable from most supermarkets. Fresh sponge fingers will not absorb the liquid.

Serve the pudding with a bowl of thick cream. It keeps well, refrigerated, for several days.

- Grease six ¾-cup capacity soufflé dishes.

- Place the milk in a saucepan with the sugar.

- Break the ladyfingers up roughly and add to the pan. Add the chocolate. Stir over a low heat until the ladyfingers have absorbed some of the milk and the chocolate is melted. It will be a thick lumpy mixture.

- Beat the eggs until frothy and gradually add the chocolate mixture. Stir well and pour into the soufflé dishes.

- Put boiling water in a baking dish so that it will reach half-way up the side of the soufflé dishes. Put the dishes in the water, and loosely cover the top of the baking dish with foil.

- Preheat the oven to 180–190°C. Bake the puddings for 15 to 20 minutes or until lightly set. Leave to stand for 5 minutes.

- Run a knife around the edge of each dish, invert the puddings onto a plate and serve with cream or ice cream.

NOTE If you intend to serve the puddings chilled, once cool turn them out onto a plate, cover with plastic wrap and refrigerate. It is very difficult to unmould them once they are very cold.

VEGETABLES

These vegetables dishes make the most of our wonderful supply of fresh produce. Choose recipes featuring vegetables that are in season, and look for firm, well-shaped produce that is rich in colour and smells sweet and fresh. These dishes can be served to accompany meat, poultry or fish, or can be served on their own as a main meal.

BEANS

Bean Shoots with Ginger   *Serves 4*

1 tablespoon peanut oil
1 onion, finely chopped
1 clove garlic, finely chopped
1 teaspoon grated fresh ginger
250 g bean shoots
½ teaspoon sugar
2 tablespoons soy sauce
salt
pepper

Bean shoots should retain some crisp texture so cook just lightly. With the ginger and soy flavour they are ideal used as a bed for a simple breast of chicken, and if you like hot food a dash of chilli sauce adds a spicy touch.

- Heat the oil in a deep frying pan or wok and add the onion. Fry, stirring, for a couple of minutes.

- Add the garlic and ginger to the pan and cook for 30 seconds. Add the bean shoots and toss for 1 minute or until they have slightly softened.

- Mix the sugar with the soy sauce, and pour around the sides of the pan. Toss to coat the vegetables, and season. The amount of salt you use will depend on whether the soy sauce is dark (highly salted) or light.

Beans with Kaiser Fleisch   *Serves 4*

500 g green stringless beans, topped
  and tailed
salt
125 g Kaiser Fleisch
freshly ground black pepper
1 teaspoon lemon juice

Kaiser Fleisch is a continental smoked bacon, which is usually bought in good delicatessens. It has a smoky flavour and firm texture. Prosciutto could also be used in the dish; the flavour will be different but equally effective with the beans.

- Bring a large saucepan of water to the boil.

- Place the beans, a third at a time, in the water. When it comes back to the boil add salt, and cook until the beans are just tender.

- Trim the rind from the Kaiser Fleisch and cut the meat into thin strips and then dice. Place in a saucepan and cook until crisp.

- Drain the beans, add the Kaiser Fleisch and any of the tasty fat around it, and season with freshly ground black pepper. Add the lemon juice, toss, and serve.

NOTE If you use prosciutto you may need to add a little butter to give added moisture to the beans, as it does not have as much fat as Kaiser Fleisch.

Beans with Sesame Seeds

Serves 4

500 g green stringless beans, topped
  and tailed
salt
2 tablespoons sesame seeds
45 g butter
squeeze of lemon juice

Although you can buy toasted sesame seeds I prefer to cook them in a dry frying pan just prior to use: the roasted nutty flavour is much more intense and marvellous with the mildness of green beans.

- Bring a large saucepan of water to the boil.

- Place the beans, a third at a time, in the water. When it comes back to the boil add salt, and cook until the beans are just tender.

- Put the sesame seeds into a dry frying pan and cook until they are brown and aromatic.

- Cut the butter into small pieces.

- Drain the beans and return to the pan. Add the butter, lemon juice and sesame seeds, and toss quickly so the beans are glazed with butter and lightly coated with seeds.

Green Beans in Tomato and Peanut Sauce

Serves 4

2 tablespoons light olive oil
1 large onion, finely diced
375 g young green beans
2 ripe tomatoes, peeled
½ cup peanuts
a good dash of Tabasco *or* chilli
  sauce
salt
freshly ground black pepper

As this dish has lots of flavour and colour it is good with any simply cooked dish, such as roast chicken, lamb or grilled steak. Use unsalted or low-salt peanuts or you will find the sauce will be too salty.

- Heat the oil in a frying pan and cook the onion gently, giving it an occasional stir, until softened.

- Put a saucepan of salted water on to boil.

- Top and tail the beans. If large, cut them into two or three pieces; you can leave the beans whole if they are baby ones. Cook the beans in the boiling water for about 3 minutes. They will not be tender at this stage.

- Chop the tomatoes roughly and add to the onion. Turn up the heat and cook for about 3 minutes or until the juices have run.

- Add the cooked beans to the tomato and onion mixture. Cover and simmer for about 5 minutes or until the beans have softened (this is one instance in which I do not recommend that beans are served crisp).

- Grind the peanuts in a food processor or blender. Add the ground peanuts to the sauce, which will then thicken. Season with Tabasco or chilli sauce and check for salt and pepper.

BROCCOLI

Broccoli with Almonds and Pimento

Serves 4

500 g broccoli
salt
60 g butter
60 g slivered almonds
200 g canned pimentos, drained
pepper

Canned pimentos, from Spain, are usually sold in the gourmet section of supermarkets or in delicatessens. They are a red capsicum, canned in a light brine and smoky in flavour.

- Bring a large saucepan of water to the boil.

- Remove the leaves from the broccoli and cut away the flower ends in small sections. Peel the stalks and cut into a few chunky pieces.

- Add the broccoli stalks and salt to the water, and cook for 1 minute. Add the broccoli florets and cook for a few minutes or until tender. Drain.

- Melt half the butter in a frying pan, add the almonds and cook, tossing, until golden to light brown.

- Cut the pimento into small dice.

- Mix the pimento into the pan with the almonds, add the remaining butter, season with salt and pepper, melt and pour over the top of the broccoli. Serve the dish quickly as broccoli fast becomes cold.

Stir-fried Broccoli

Serves 4

375 g broccoli
2 tablespoons light olive oil
1 tablespoon very finely shredded
  fresh ginger
1 large clove garlic, finely chopped
⅓ cup water *or* chicken stock
salt
freshly ground black pepper

A great source of vitamins, broccoli should be cooked quickly and served a little green and crisp, making stir-frying the ideal way to cook it. While this dish has Asian flavours, it can still be teamed with a Western-based meal of meat or poultry. It also makes a delicious but simple lunch when served with rice.

- Cut the broccoli florets from the stalks. Peel the stalks and cut them into slices.

- Heat the oil in a large frying pan or wok and fry the ginger and garlic for a minute or until aromatic.

- Add the broccoli and stir-fry, tossing and turning it in the garlic and ginger.

- Tip in the water or stock and leave to cook for a couple of minutes. As soon as the broccoli is just tender season with salt and pepper and serve.

CABBAGE

Shredded Cabbage with Bacon   *Serves 4*

½ medium-sized cabbage
salt
4 rashers bacon, rind removed
30 g butter
1 teaspoon sugar
freshly ground black pepper

When carefully cooked, cabbage can be a sweet-tasting and very flavoursome vegetable. This particular dish with its bacon flavour is good with pork or chicken. I have on occasions served it as a light lunch dish: cooking and then cooling the cabbage and wrapping it in layers of buttery filo, before baking it like a long strudel and serving it with melted butter.

- Discard any wilted or large outside cabbage leaves and cut the cabbage into shreds, which do not have to be very fine. Wash and drain. Place in a saucepan with sufficient water to cover the base, and season with salt. Cook, covered, for about 8 to 10 minutes or until tender.

- Cut the bacon into thin strips and fry in a dry frying pan until crisp. Do not drain as the fat is used in the dish.

- Drain the cabbage well.

- Put the butter into the same saucepan with the sugar, and melt. Add the cabbage and bacon and any fat from the frying pan. Toss until everything is hot and well mixed. Remove from the heat, season with the freshly ground black pepper, and serve.

Cabbage in a Light Curry Sauce   *Serves 4*

½ small cabbage
1 onion
3 tablespoons light olive oil
2 teaspoons mustard seeds
1 teaspoon curry powder
1 tomato, peeled and roughly
  chopped
½ teaspoon sugar
1 cup coconut milk
chopped peanuts for garnishing
  (optional)

Served with a bowl of rice, this very flavoursome and moist dish could make a light meal. As an accompaniment serve it alongside a simple dish that does not have much sauce.

- Finely shred the cabbage.

- Cut the onion in half and then into segments.

- Heat half the oil in a large saucepan or a wok, add the cabbage and onion and fry until wilted, tossing them as they cook. Remove to a bowl and put to one side.

- Heat the remaining oil and fry the mustard seeds until they begin to change colour. Add the curry powder and fry for a few seconds before mixing in the tomato, sugar and coconut milk. Cook gently for about 5 minutes.

- Return the cabbage and onion mixture to the saucepan or wok and leave to simmer for a couple of minutes. Serve plain or with some chopped peanuts on top.

CARROTS

Sautéd Carrot and Onion

Serves 4

375 g baby carrots
salt
30 g butter
1 tablespoon oil
1 onion, cut into thin half-slices
1 teaspoon sugar
pepper

A combination dish of glazed carrots and onions, the vegetables are both sweet and flavoursome and will go with almost any meat or poultry.

- Scrub the carrots, trim the ends, place in boiling salted water and cook uncovered until tender.

- Heat the butter and oil in a saucepan and add the onion slices. Sauté until wilted.

- Drain the carrots and add to the onion. Add the sugar and pepper, mix, and continue cooking for about 5 minutes or until glazed and golden.

Carrot and Potato Purée

Serves 4

500 g potatoes, peeled
250 g carrots, peeled
salt
30 g butter
2 tablespoons cream
dash of milk (if necessary)
2 tablespoons finely chopped fresh
  chives *or* parsley
freshly ground black pepper

A magical transformation takes place when carrot is puréed with potatoes. This creamy dish will have an attractive pale, pinky-orange tinge and is lighter to eat than plain mashed potato. It is particularly good for mopping up a delicious sauce.

- Cut the potatoes into quarters if large; if small leave whole.
- Slice the carrots thickly.
- Place the potato and carrot in a saucepan, cover with water, add salt and bring to the boil. Cook gently, covered, until tender. Drain.
- Either mash the vegetables or put through a Mouli.
- Add the butter while the purée is warm. Add the cream, stir, and return to the saucepan to warm again. If too thick, add more cream or a dash of milk.
- Stir the chives through the purée just before serving, and season with pepper. Check for salt at the finish.

Cauliflower with Cheese and Cream Sauce   *Serves 4*

375 g cauliflower
30 g butter
1 tablespoon light olive oil *or*
  vegetable oil
salt
pepper
¾ cup water
½ cup cream
¾ cup grated St Claire *or* Jarlsberg
  cheese

This is a short-cut recipe for making a very rich and creamy cheese sauce for not only cauliflower but for any dish that lends itself to it.

• Cut the cauliflower into quarters and then across into thick slices. Begin at the stalk end and as you get to the florets cut it a little thicker.

• Melt the butter and heat the oil in a frying pan.

• When the pan is hot, add the cauliflower and toss for a couple of minutes or until tinged with gold.

• Season the cauliflower, add the water and cook until the water has almost evaporated and the cauliflower is tender. If too crisp, add more water. When ready, tilt to remove any excess liquid.

• Stir the cream and cheese together. Pour over the cauliflower and mix gently. The cheese will melt almost immediately and form a sauce. Once melted serve immediately; if you leave it any longer the cheese can be come stringy.

Sliced Cauliflower with Pine Nuts   *Serves 4*

4 tablespoons light olive oil
30 g pine nuts
1 medium-sized onion, roughly
  chopped
500 g cauliflower
salt
pepper
1 cup water *or* light chicken stock

Slicing the cauliflower before cooking ensures a very fast dish but be careful not to over-cook.

• Heat half the oil in a frying pan. Add the pine nuts and cook, stirring, until golden brown. Drain on kitchen paper.

• Add the onion to the pan. There should be sufficient oil; if not add a little more. Cook until wilted.

• While the onion is cooking, cut the cauliflower into quarters and then across into thin slices. Begin at the stalk end and as you get to the florets cut it a little thicker.

• Turn the heat up under the pan. Add the remaining oil and the cauliflower, and toss for a few minutes.

• Season the cauliflower with salt and pepper and add the water. Cook without a lid. By the time the water has almost evaporated the cauliflower should be tender.

• Scatter the pine nuts on the cauliflower, and serve.

NOTE If you use stock the cauliflower will be cream rather than white in colour; it will have a better flavour but not such an attractive appearance.

EGGPLANT

Eggplant Baked with Cheese   *Serves 4*

2 medium-sized eggplant
1 teaspoon salt
45 g butter
1 tablespoon plain flour
½ cup cream
1 tablespoon French mustard
salt
freshly ground black pepper
2 tomatoes, sliced
½ cup breadcrumbs made from
  stale bread
½ cup grated tasty *or* Parmesan
  cheese

This is one of the few dishes in which eggplant, even if not very fresh, does not require salting. This is because the eggplant is boiled rather than fried or baked; any bitterness cooks away in the water. It is quite a mild-flavoured dish and can be served as a first course or as an accompaniment.

If you make this dish at the last moment, and the eggplant and sauce are still hot, you can just grill the topping to heat it through before serving.

- Preheat the oven to 180°C.

- Peel the eggplant and cut into bite-sized pieces.

- Put the chopped eggplant into a saucepan, cover with water, add a teaspoon of salt and bring to the boil. Cook for about 5 minutes or until tender. Drain, reserving the cooking liquid.

- Melt the butter in a saucepan, add the flour and fry for a few minutes. Add ½ cup of the reserved cooking liquid with the cream and bring to the boil, stirring constantly. Mix in the French mustard, and taste for seasoning.

- Place the eggplant in a shallow baking dish and pour the sauce over the top.

- Arrange the sliced tomato on top of the sauce. Season.

- Mix the breadcrumbs with the cheese and scatter over the tomato. Bake for about 20 minutes.

Eggplant Chips   *Serves 4*

500 g eggplant, peeled
salt
1 cup milk
½ cup plain flour
peanut oil
pepper

Apart from being a side vegetable, these crunchy eggplant strips can be nibbled as an appetiser. Be sure to buy very firm, shiny, fresh eggplant so the chips will be sweet and not bitter.

- Cut the eggplant into thick slices and across into strips to make chips. Scatter with salt and leave to stand for about 20 minutes. Rinse and drain well on kitchen paper or a tea towel.

- Put the eggplant chips into a basin, cover with the milk, stand for 5 minutes and drain.

- Place the flour in a paper bag. Add the eggplant chips, a few at a time, and shake well. Hold the top of the bag so no flour escapes. As they are done, place the chips in a colander so the excess flour falls away.

- Heat a medium-sized saucepan with enough peanut oil to come half-way up the sides, or use a deep fryer. When the oil is so hot that a chip sizzles instantly when tested, add a handful of the eggplant chips and cook for about 1 minute or until golden. Fry all the eggplant chips, a handful at a time, and drain on kitchen paper. Season generously with salt and pepper.

NOTE The eggplant chips do not keep crisp for long so they should be done at the last minute. If you wish, you can scatter freshly grated Parmesan cheese on top before serving.

LETTUCE

Sautéd Lettuce and Onion

Serves 4

45 g butter
2 medium-sized onions, cut into
  thin half-slices
1 medium-sized lettuce (preferably
  iceberg)
½ cup chicken stock *or* water
salt
pepper

The outside lettuce leaves can be used, provided they are not too tough, but include some of the softer inner leaves as well. Iceberg lettuce is the most successful in this dish, although a soft butter lettuce can be used; you may need two if they are small ones. The texture of cooked lettuce is firmer than cooked spinach or silverbeet and the colour is pale.

- Melt the butter in a large frying pan, add the onion and cook over a medium heat until wilted.

- Discard the tough outside leaves of the lettuce. Cut the lettuce into halves, place them flat on a board and cut down into thin slices. Add to the pan with the onion and cook until limp.

- Add the chicken stock, salt and pepper and cook over a high heat for about 5 minutes or until the lettuce and onion are tender.

ONION

Onion Cooked with Fresh Herbs

Serves 4

4 onions
45 g butter
1 tablespoon light olive oil
1 teaspoon sugar
¼ cup finely chopped fresh parsley
2 teaspoons finely chopped fresh
  thyme
1 teaspoon finely chopped fresh
  rosemary
¼ cup chicken stock *or* water

This dish is perfect with steak or, if you love the sweet flavour of fried onions, you can just pile it on some fresh warm toast.

- Cut each of the onions in half and then into thin wedges. You don't need to separate these as they will automatically come apart as they cook.

- Melt the butter with the oil in a saucepan. Add the onion and let it cook over a medium heat, stirring occasionally, until wilted and golden. (Let the onion pick up colour, which will mean that the dish will have more flavour and added sweetness.)

- Add the sugar and fry for a minute.

- Mix in the parsley, thyme and rosemary.

- Add the stock and bring to the boil. Cook until just a little juice remains around the onion.

Onion Cooked in Wine with Pine Nuts

Serves 4

4 large onions
45 g butter
1 teaspoon sugar
salt
pepper
½ cup dry white *or* red wine
2 tablespoons pine nuts
2 teaspoons oil

Either white or red wine can be used in this dish. The flavour and colour will be different but the dish will still be sweet and tasty.

- Cut the onions into halves. Cut the halves into sections to make wedges, rather like an apple. You should get four wedges from each onion half.

- Melt the butter in a saucepan and add the onion. Cook over a moderately high heat until the onion is coated with butter.

- Add the sugar, salt and pepper to the pan and cook until tinged with gold. Add the wine and cook over a moderate heat until the onion has softened and the wine has evaporated. You will have just a little juice around the onion.

- Put the pine nuts and oil in a small frying pan and cook until the pine nuts are golden brown. Drain.

- Add the pine nuts to the onion, stir gently to mix, and serve; or you can serve the onion and scatter the nuts on top.

NOTE If the liquid cooks away and the onion is still too firm, place a lid on the pan and leave it to sweat for about 5 minutes.

POTATO AND RICE

Baked Potato Slices

Serves 4

500 g old potatoes, unpeeled
45 g butter
1 tablespoon virgin olive oil *or* light
 olive oil
3 cloves garlic, unpeeled
salt
pepper

These are as crunchy as chips but a lot easier to make as you can leave them in the oven while you are preparing the rest of the dinner. The garlic lightly flavours the butter and oil and then lingers on the potato. The potato slices complement a simple lamb main course.

- Wash the unpeeled potatoes well and cut into thick slices.

- Melt the butter, add the oil and heat in a small saucepan. Brush on the base of a shallow baking dish. Put the potato slices in a single layer into the dish and brush the top of each one with more of the butter and oil mixture. Trickle any remaining mixture on top.

- Tuck the garlic into the pan.

- Preheat the oven to 180°C. Season the potato generously with salt and pepper and bake for about 30 minutes or until tender.

NOTE If you want the potato slices very crisp leave a little longer. You may need to turn the slices over before a golden crust forms.

Cream-cooked Potatoes

Serves 4

500 g small new potatoes
salt
½ cup sour cream
2 tablespoons finely chopped fresh
 chives
pepper

As these potatoes are quite rich, serve with a simply cooked dish. You can use either thick or thin sour cream.

- Peel the potatoes. (If they are not small cut into halves or quarters.) Cover with cold water, add salt, and gently cook, covered, until tender. Drain.

- Return the potatoes to the same saucepan and pour the sour cream over the top.

- Cook for about 5 minutes or until the cream becomes thick around the potatoes (it sometimes becomes oily but this is not a concern).

- Scatter the chives on top of the potatoes, add plenty of pepper, and shake the pan or stir gently to coat them. Serve.

Sautéd Potato Cubes
Serves 4

750 g potatoes, peeled
2 tablespoons virgin olive oil *or*
  light olive oil
30 g butter
salt
pepper
2 teaspoons freshly chopped
  rosemary *or* a little dried rosemary

This dish can be made with either old or new potatoes; the former have a soft, creamy texture while the latter are firmer and may take longer to cook.

- Cut the potatoes into large dice.

- Heat the oil and butter in a large frying pan and when foaming add the potato. Cook for about 20 minutes, giving an occasional stir so it cooks evenly.

- Season with salt and pepper, scatter the rosemary on top, and serve.

Sautéd Potato with Garlic and Parsley
Serves 4

750 g potatoes, peeled
30 g butter
2 tablespoons virgin olive oil
2 cloves garlic, finely chopped *or*
  crushed
3 tablespoons freshly chopped
  parsley
salt
freshly ground black pepper

This dish can be made with either old or new potatoes. The old potatoes have a soft creamy texture; the new ones remain firmer and take a little longer to cook. To make the cubes very crisp, the salt is added at the finish when the potato is cooked rather than at the beginning.

- Cut the potatoes into chunky bite-sized pieces.

- Heat the butter and oil in a large frying pan and when sizzling hot add the potato. Stir until it is coated. Cook the potato for about 15 to 20 minutes, giving it a stir every so often so all sides become golden and crisp.

- Mix the garlic with the parsley.

- When the potato is cooked, scatter the garlic and parsley mixture and plenty of salt and pepper on top.

Potatoes Lyonnaise
Serves 4

750 g small potatoes, peeled
salt
30 g butter
2 tablespoons light olive oil
2 onions, cut into thin half-slices
pepper

The secret of this dish is to keep the heat to such a level that the potato and onion cook at a constant moderate heat. The onion is soft and tinged with gold, but not too dark, and the potato is slightly crisp and golden.

- Cut the potatoes into halves; if large cut them into quarters. Place in a saucepan, cover with water and season with salt. Cook, covered, over a low heat until tender. Drain.

- Heat the butter and oil in a large frying pan and add the onion. Cook for a few minutes until wilted.

- Add the potato to the frying pan and continue cooking until the onion is golden and the potato fried on the outside. Season with pepper and a little more salt if you wish.

Potatoes with Paprika and Capsicum Sauce
Serves 4

750 g small potatoes, peeled
salt
1 large red *or* yellow *or* green
  capsicum
30 g butter
2 tablespoons light olive oil
1 tablespoon ground sweet paprika
½ cup sour cream
extra salt
pepper

You will obtain the sweetest flavour by using red or yellow capsicum in this dish; green capsicum will give it a much stronger taste.

- Place the potatoes in a saucepan, cover with water, add salt and cook gently until tender. Drain. Cut into halves.

- Cut the capsicum into halves, discard the seeds and cut the flesh into small dice.

- Heat the butter and oil in a frying pan, add the capsicum and cook over a medium heat until softened.

- Add the paprika to the pan, stir, and fry for about 30 seconds. Add the sour cream and bring to the boil.

- Add the potato to the frying pan and stir to coat with the mixture. Cook until quite warm, season with a little salt and pepper, and serve.

Rice with Sultanas and Almonds
Serves 6

2 tablespoons light olive oil
1 onion, finely chopped
1½ cups long-grain rice
3 cups water *or* chicken stock
1 stick cinnamon (the size of a
  finger)
4 tablespoons sultanas
salt
pepper
60 g slivered almonds
45 g butter

A good accompaniment to a chicken dish or curry, this dish could also be served with some vegetables on the side in a meatless meal.

- Heat the oil in a heavy-based saucepan and add the onion. Cook for about 5 minutes or until softened.

- Add the rice and cook, stirring, until the grains are mostly opaque.

- Add the water, push the cinnamon stick into the pan, add the sultanas and bring to the boil. Season (this will depend on whether you use water or seasoned stock). Cover, and cook over a very low heat until the liquid has been absorbed and the rice is tender. It takes about 15 to 20 minutes.

- While the rice is cooking, toast the slivered almonds in a dry frying pan until golden.

- When the rice is ready, add the butter and slivered almonds, and toss gently with two forks to fluff up the rice.

PUMPKIN

Baked Pumpkin Cubes with Sesame Seeds   *Serves 4*

1 kg blue *or* butternut pumpkin
1 tablespoon peanut oil *or* light
  olive oil
30 g butter
salt
pepper
2 tablespoons sesame seeds

This dish needs a dry baking pumpkin such as a blue or a butternut.

- Peel the pumpkin and remove any seeds. Cut into small neat cubes. Place in a shallow ovenproof dish in which they will fit in one layer.

- Trickle the oil over the top of the pumpkin and dot with butter. Season with salt and pepper.

- Preheat the oven to 180°C. Bake the pumpkin for about 15 minutes, turning the cubes over several times.

- Scatter the sesame seeds over the top of the pumpkin and continue cooking for another 10 minutes or until the pumpkin is tender.

Pumpkin Parcels with Coconut Milk and Basil *Serves 4*

500 g butternut *or* a rich baking
  pumpkin
a little oil
1 clove garlic, sliced
1 small onion, finely diced
salt
freshly ground black pepper
dash of Tabasco *or* chilli sauce
½ cup coconut milk
8 large fresh basil leaves

Bake these aromatic parcels in the oven, or put them around the edge of the barbecue next time you're entertaining outside.

- Preheat the oven to 180°C.

- Peel, seed and cut the pumpkin into bite-sized dice.

- Cut four sheets of foil, each one large enough to make a parcel. If the foil is thin use two layers. Lightly oil the foil on the uppermost side.

- Put some pumpkin on each sheet of foil. Divide the garlic and the onion between the sheets.

- Season the vegetables with salt, pepper and Tabasco.

- To make the first parcel, gather up the sides of the foil and seal them, making a tuck along the top but leaving an opening. Pour some coconut milk into the opening, put in a couple of basil leaves and seal the top. Repeat the process to complete the remaining parcels.

- Bake on a tray for about 25 minutes or until the pumpkin is soft.

SNOW PEAS

Snow Peas

Serves 4

250 g snow peas
1 teaspoon salt
1 teaspoon sugar
1 tablespoon light olive oil

This quantity of snow peas should be plenty for four people as there is no wastage and as a rule snow peas are served in smaller quantities than other vegetables.

- Top and tail the snow peas.

- Bring a saucepan of water to the boil, season with the salt and sugar, and add the peas. Cook for a couple of minutes and drain.

- Return the snow peas to the pan. Add the oil and shake so the snow peas are shiny and coated with oil.

Sauté of Snow Peas with Ginger and Chilli

Serves 4

250 g snow peas
2 tablespoons light olive oil
1.25-cm piece fresh ginger, cut into thin matchsticks
2 cloves garlic, finely diced or sliced
1 small fresh chilli, deseeded and chopped
¼ cup water
salt
1 teaspoon dark sesame oil

This crunchy, brightly coloured dish can be enjoyed with chicken or meat, or with rice as part of a mixed vegetable selection.

- Pull away the top thread on the snow peas.

- Heat the light olive oil in a wok or frying pan. Add the ginger, garlic and chilli and stir-fry for a few seconds. It should smell very spicy. Don't let the mixture burn.

- Add the snow peas and toss quickly for a minute. Tip the water in around the edges to create steam and cook for another minute. Season with a good pinch of salt.

- Add the sesame oil, mix through and serve.

SQUASH

Baby Squash and Mushrooms   *Serves 4*

375 g baby yellow squash
salt
freshly ground black pepper
30 g butter
125 g small mushrooms
1 clove garlic, chopped
squeeze of lemon juice
2 tablespoons thick cream *or* crème
  fraîche
1 tablespoon finely chopped fresh
  parsley *or* chives

Yellow squash, sometimes called 'custard squash', are delicious if tiny, but a bit watery when very large. Their golden colour and unique shape make them attractive as a side dish, and their buttery mild flavour teams with chicken or simply cooked meat dishes.

- Cook the squash in boiling, salted water until just tender. Drain, cool slightly, cut into halves if small or quarters if large and return to the saucepan. Season with pepper.

- Melt the butter in a frying pan, add the mushrooms and garlic and cook over a high heat for a couple of minutes until the mushrooms are tender. Add a squeeze of lemon juice. Tip the mushroom mixture into the saucepan with the squash. Do not add any liquid around the mushroom as the dish will become too watery.

- When ready to serve, mix in the cream, and warm through. Add the parsley or chives. Serve immediately.

NOTE If you cook the squash and mushroom in the cream for too long the squash will give out liquid and the sauce will become very thin.

Baby Squash with Butter and Rosemary   *Serves 4*

375 g baby yellow squash
salt
30 g butter
2 teaspoons finely chopped fresh
  rosemary
pepper

These little yellow squash are also known as custard marrow and are only good when very fresh; as they age they become slightly bitter. Try to buy them only about 5 cm across.

- Trim away the small stalk on top of the squash. Place the squash in a saucepan, cover with water, and add salt. Cook, covered, for about 8 to 10 minutes or until tender. Drain.

- Melt the butter in the same saucepan, add the rosemary and pepper, and return the squash. Toss so they are coated with butter, and serve.

TOMATOES

Tiny Tomatoes with Basil, Olives and Capers   *Serves 4*

2 cloves garlic
2 tablespoons virgin olive oil
250 g cherry tomatoes
salt
freshly ground black pepper
a pinch of sugar
⅓ cup shredded fresh basil leaves
1 tablespoon rinsed and chopped
  capers
⅓ cup ligurian *or* niçoise olives

Brightly coloured and bursting with flavour, these tomatoes can be served alongside any plain meat dish as a marvellously pungent sauce. Tiny tom tomatoes, cherry tomatoes, cocktail tomatoes: call them what you wish, any baby tomato is suitable for this dish.

The most important part in the cooking of this dish is getting the timing right; the skins of the tomatoes should be soft and the flesh cooked – too long over the heat will cause the seeds to spill out. This is not a dish you can prepare in advance and keep warm; it needs to be cooked quickly and served immediately.

- Put the garlic and oil into a saucepan. Heat until the oil is just bubbling on the edge, remove from the heat and leave it stand while you cut the tomatoes into halves.

- Remove the garlic from the oil and discard. Heat the oil again, add the tomato halves and season with salt, pepper and sugar.

- When the tomato has softened and the mixture is bubbling, add the basil, capers and olives. Shake gently to mix and heat for about 30 seconds. Serve immediately.

Garlic-scented Tomatoes   *Serves 4*

4 ripe tomatoes
salt
pepper
sugar
2 cloves garlic
30 g butter

The small garlic slivers that are inserted into the tomato as it cooks, adding a delicate garlic flavour to the tomato flesh, can be left in or you can quickly pull them out before serving.

- Cut each tomato into halves and season with salt, pepper and a dash of sugar.

- Cut the garlic into slivers. Insert a generous piece in each tomato half, pushing it well down into the centre.

- Place the tomato halves in a shallow ovenproof dish and place the smallest dot of butter on top of each one.

- Preheat the oven to 180°C. Bake the tomato halves for about 12 to 15 minutes or until soft but not breaking.

ZUCCHINI

Crispy Zucchini Strips

Serves 4

500 g zucchini
½ cup seasoned plain flour
peanut oil
3 tablespoons grated Parmesan
  cheese

*Although a delicious side dish, this can also be an appetiser.
The zucchini strips need to be done at the very last moment as
they will become limp quickly. However, they can be cut and
coated with flour 30 minutes before cooking.*

- Remove the ends from the zucchini. Cut into long thick
  slices and then thick strips so they are about the size of
  potato chips.

- Place the zucchini strips, a few at a time, in a paper bag.
  Shake the bag to coat the strips. Remove to a colander as
  you do them so the excess flour falls away. Transfer to a
  plate and separate them out.

- Heat a medium-sized saucepan with enough peanut oil to
  come half-way up the sides, or use a deep fryer. When the oil
  is so hot that a zucchini strip sizzles instantly when tested,
  add a handful of them and cook for 1 minute or until crisp
  on the outside and cooked through. Fry all the strips and
  drain on kitchen paper.

- Scatter the grated Parmesan cheese on the zucchini strips,
  and serve.

Sautéd Zucchini

Serves 4

8 small zucchini
45 g butter
1 tablespoon virgin olive oil *or* light
  olive oil
salt
pepper
1 tablespoon water

*Boiled or even steamed zucchini can be very uninteresting and
tasteless because of the high water content; fried until crispy on
the outside but still soft inside it becomes much more
flavoursome. The dish requires just a little watching to make
sure the zucchini cooks through before it becomes golden; for
the best result do not have the heat too high and choose small
zucchini.*

- Cut the ends from each zucchini and halve lengthwise.

- Heat the butter and oil in a frying pan in which the zucchini
  will fit in one layer. Add the zucchini, cut side down, and
  season.

- Cook the zucchini over a medium heat until golden. Turn
  over and cook the other side until golden. When you turn
  the zucchini over, add the tablespoon of water to the pan.
  Cooking the vegetable should take 10 to 15 minutes and it
  should be tender but not too soft.

NOTE If you find the zucchini halves are still too crisp you can
put a lid on the pan for a couple of minutes to sweat them at
the finish.

Sautéd Grated Zucchini
Serves 4

750 g zucchini
fine table salt
45 g butter
freshly ground black pepper
1 medium-sized ripe tomato

This dish is fast if you have a food processor with a grating facility; if not, grate by hand on a coarse grater.

- Remove the ends from the zucchini, and grate the zucchini coarsely in a food processor or by hand.

- Place the zucchini on a dinner plate in layers, scattering each layer with fine table salt. Leave to rest for 10 minutes. Squeeze the zucchini to remove as much liquid as possible.

- Melt the butter in a frying pan, add the zucchini and pepper, and toss for 2 to 3 minutes or until softened.

- Cut the tomato into very small dice (there is no need to peel or seed it). Add to the zucchini, and cook for 1 minute or until the tomato has softened.

NOTE Although a fair amount of salt is scattered on the zucchini, almost all of this comes away when you squeeze it. Not so much will come out if coarse kitchen salt is used, so be sure to use fine table salt.

Zucchini Sautéd with Tomato
Serves 4

6 baby zucchini (8 if very small)
45 g butter
1 tablespoon light olive oil
1 tablespoon tomato paste
½ cup water
salt
pepper
1 large clove garlic, unpeeled

Large zucchini are not particularly successful in this dish, so use the baby ones for the best flavour and appearance.

- Remove the ends from the zucchini, and cut each one in half lengthwise.

- Heat the butter and oil in a large frying pan and add the zucchini, cut side down. Cook over a medium heat for about 8 minutes or until they have slightly softened, turning them over once.

- Mix the tomato paste with the water, salt and pepper in a basin and pour over the zucchini.

- Add the garlic to the pan.

- Cook the zucchini until the sauce has reduced to a thick syrup around them and remove the garlic before serving.

INDEX